Sign Design

Graphics • Materials • Techniques

Sign Design

Graphics
Materials
Techniques

Mitzi Sims

THAMES AND HUDSON

For Anthony

First published in Great Britain in 1991 by
Thames and Hudson Ltd, London

This book was designed and produced by
John Calmann & King Ltd, London

Designed by Wade Greenwood

Printed in Singapore by Toppan Printing Company Ltd

Title page illustrations:
Page 2
see pages 138, 106, 108

Page 3
see pages 156, 153, 95

Acknowledgements
I would like to thank everyone who has been so kind in helping me with this project. Specifically: Jim Bodoh, James Woudhuysen, Ken Garland, Rufus Segar; Nicolete Gray, David Kindersley, Lida Lopez Cardozo, Richard Kindersley, Chris Ludlow, Jamie Wood, John Wood. Also, from the UK: Victoria Thornton, Alan Fletcher, Theo Crosby, Richard Seymour, Colin Porter, Terry Trickett, David Brown, Don Dunthorne, Peter Tipton, John Frank, Michael Glickman. Also, from the US: Sarah Speare, Lance Wyman, Debra Nichols, Coco Raynes, Keith Helmetag, Rebecca Rose and Paul Arthur (Canada). Thank you too to John Calmann King Ltd, my publishers, specifically Paula Iley, Sophie Collins and Liz Thussu.

Contents

Introduction

◀ Douglas Doolittle enjoys working
with construction materials such as
brick, used here in a sign for a beer
hall called *Nessa* in Shibuya-ku,
Tokyo. I felt that one of the prerequisites
of design was not only to convey the
name (a feeling for desert thirst) but
also to emphasize the beauty of the
wall that supported it. The illuminated
sign is also made from steel, sand and
brass.

Introduction

▶ This striking sign, clearly legible by night or day, was designed by Henrion Ludlow and Schmidt as part of their worldwide corporate identity scheme for Coopers and Lybrand, international accountants and management consultants with more than four hundred offices in one hundred countries.

This book is about the design, production, implementation, maintenance and appreciation of signs. All signs are man-made and designed to communicate, and a number of different forms of signing exist from which designers can draw inspiration. Many types of designers and design organizations are represented in this book, and the illustrated examples vary from billboard art to sophisticated electronic systems.

Signing terms

Clarification of the use of language is important as it allows all the people involved in the signing process – designers, architects, planners, developers, manufacturers, clients and users – to understand each other. Designers are notorious for making up new words and attaching coded meanings to existing ones. Precision should remedy this situation, detering the application of inappropriate labels and avoiding confusion and unnecessary complications.

'Signing', 'signs', 'sign-posts', 'sign systems' and so on are the main words used in signing, and signing is a specific aspect of environmental graphic design. *Signage* is not a 'real' word. It is a term first used by Paul Arthur, a pioneer of 'wayfinding' (discussed in Chapter 3). The word established what he describes as a 'mindset': that problems in finding one's way around an environment can be solved by putting up signs. The term is intentionally not used by the US Society of Environmental Graphic Designers (SEGD) and the British Standards Institute (BSI).

The job of an environmental graphic designer is defined by the SEGD.

The environmental graphic designer plans, designs and specifies sign systems and other forms of visual communication in the built and natural environment. Environmental graphic design serves three basic functions: to assist users in negotiating through space, by identifying, directing and informing to visually enhance the environment and to protect the safety of the public.

In creating graphic elements for a building or a site, environmental graphic designers analyse the architectural, cultural, and aesthetic factors to meet the needs of both clients and users. Their design process is informed by their visual communication skills and knowledge of appropriate materials, methods and technologies.

Environmental graphic designers are professionals who are qualified by their skills, education, and experience. Their activities are guided by the Code of Ethics established for the profession [by the SEGD] as well as related laws, regulations, and contractual obligations.

▶ Vignelli Associates have incorporated the directory graphics into the concierge desk, in the lobby of this Park Avenue office building in New York.

The signing boom

The late 1980s and early 90s are exciting times for the sign industry, for signing is no longer an amalgam of fragmented, old-fashioned, uncoordinated cottage and craft industries as it was ten years ago, but rather an industry which is rapidly responding to the climate of change. Developments in company structure, equipment and technology have transformed many signmakers into industrialists involved in engineering, electronics and computer-aided design and manufacturing techniques. Yet the industry still accommodates small companies supplying local needs, and individual craftspeople whose skills are in constant demand. In the US, the UK and Europe, the sign industry has never been healthier, and there has never been so much interest, discussion and debate. Newspaper articles and television programmes, as well as design journals, are now looking at signs. This year sees the launching of a major bi-monthly signing magazine in Australia. All forward-looking European signing businesses are discussing the increased competition and opportunities that 1992 and the more liberated European market will afford.

In the US in 1988, clients of the four hundred or so SEGD members spent between $150 and $200 million on signing. Clients spent an average of $450,000 annually on signs, with a high of $1.3 million and a low of $100,000. The dollar breakdown of sign types was approximately 35% exterior illuminated, 25% exterior non-illuminated, 25% interior (plastic/wood/stone), 10% interior (metal) and 10% interior (illuminated/electrical). Three-quarters of SEGD members reported that they anticipated a rise in volume. The distribution of work fell into the following categories: 42% institutional, 36% corporate, 7% government, 6% retail, 5% transportation and 4% cultural (approximate percentages).

Very little information and few statistics are available on the UK industry, partly due to its rapid expansion and development in the last ten years. However, the total market is estimated to be between £180 and £200 million per annum, and there are at least 2500 signmakers. With the possible exception of off-the-peg systems, the whole signing area in the UK is less mature than in the US. Signing is often considered part of the overall design job, and not a distinct problem. Few firms specialize in signing or even in environmental graphics. Signing is not thought of as a suitable subject for academic pursuit (although the Central School in London must be excluded from this generalization). The UK also lacks a professional design body that is exclusively for environmental graphic design, such as the SEGD in the US.

The design challenge

Signing is, however, beginning to be seen by some designers as a specific area of design, not simply the ignored poor cousin of other design disciplines, the 'treacherous art, lying in the no-man's land between architecture and graphic design' (Jock Kinneir, 1980). Specifically, although Deborah Sussman notes the 'general lack of awareness that environmental graphic design is a field of endeavour and a discipline as serious as any other,' it appears that architects are beginning to realize the creative opportunities that arise when working with environmental graphic designers, as evidenced at Solana, a business park complex in Texas (discussed in Chapter 3). The exciting pace of developments, and the academic research in wayfinding, may yet accelerate awareness and acceptance.

Designers are taking up the creative challenge of designing exotic and exuberant signs for their clients. For many designers this is an opportunity for investigating a new field, experimenting with original concepts, creating an object of beauty and permanently contributing to an environment. In the words of Peter

Tipton, chairman of the British Sign Association, 'the sign industry is now *design*– rather than manufacturer–led.'

Sign manufacturers, assisted and supported by suppliers and stockists, are becoming increasingly quick to respond to the needs of the designer, and keen to nurture and develop a close relationship with him or her. John Haliday, Marketing Director of sign manufacturers A.C. Edwards, suggests that 'it is incumbent upon the industry to provide a more comprehensive level of service to our customers, and that should mean a far greater involvement by sign manufacturers in the whole design process.' This book gives the designer the information necessary to make practical, creative decisions. It also attempts to deepen appreciation and stimulate further interest in the subject, allowing creative freedom to accompany professional responsibility.

Who is the designer?

The designer is the person who has the responsibility for making design decisions it is not assumed that the designer is an experienced professional. He or she may be an individual who is designing a simple sign for a small shop, or a professional designer within a team, with responsibility for signing a large, multilevel building complex. In the past, architects considered signing work an unwelcome, unbudgeted afterthought to their buildings, or signs were commissioned by traditional independent signwriters. Today, much of the range of professional sign work is undertaken by graphic and interior designers.

This development has provided a wealth of creative sign work which immeasurably enhances the built environment. The problem, however, is that graphic and interior designers, who have their own areas of expertise, are not taught the specific skills necessary to design signs.

◄ Traditionally, typefaces have been divided into the categories shown here.

Old face
Plantin

Modern
Bodoni

Transitional
Baskerville

Egyptian
Egyptienne

Old style
Times

Sans serif
Futura

History

This section gives a brief history of letters and alphabets and their suitability for signing, followed by a short discussion on architectural lettering and signs. It is included to provide a mental timescale, and to promote the consideration of present design projects as part of a continuum. The visual study of history may suggest unusual solutions to current design problems.

The history of letters and alphabets

The history of letters and alphabets began in 3,000 BC with the modification of early pictograms and the abstractions of recognizable images and drawings into signs and ultimately letterforms. The development of the form and style of individual characters over the centuries has been influenced by the evolution of writing, carving and printing. The

Unfortunately, a great deal of bad signing exists as testimony to this. Signing appears to be deceptively simple, whereas om fact it is usually a complex design matter requiring distinct and diverse skills.

Signing skills are often assumed to be an extension and application of graphic design. This is emphatically not the case: signing is part of environmental graphic design, although the definition of what an environmental graphic designer actually is and does is part of a debate even within the profession. Beyond any doubt, however, the design of signs requires a truly multidisciplinary approach. Massimo Vignelli, one of the most influential designers of our time, considers that an environmental graphic designer should have the following qualities: 'Discipline: to know about type, materials, manufacturing, installation. Appropriateness: to search for the solution that is specific to the problem. To know

about scale, materials and dignity of expression. To know about history and about our time, to avoid fads, and create lasting beauty.'

It is no surprise that the Society of Environmental Graphic Designers Education Foundation (SEGDEF) has found that there are no programmes or curricula to teach environmental graphic design, and that 90 per cent of employers cannot find qualified entry-level designers. SEGDEF is currently developing a model curriculum for use in US schools in an attempt to help solve the present crisis. In the UK no such initiatives exist. As the design of signs is a relatively new area, and since education in the subject is lacking, experience is key to the successful completion of projects for individual designers. Throughout this book the experiences and opinions of leading international design and technical professionals provide an insight into all aspects of the subject.

◄ At Pompeii, one of the best preserved signs is this hand-painted election notice, with superb lettering that has survived for nearly two thousand years and is now protected behind glass.

► All the signs in The Conran Shop, London, are unique. This impressive directory, made from a carved cherrywood panel, stands over two metres high. The lettering is screenprinted in dark green.

Industrial Revolution brought mass production, and towards the end of the nineteenth century mechanized typesetting was invented. This and photocomposition, often referred to as phototypesetting, have resulted in a considerable simplification of the actual characters and forms of letters themselves.

Photocomposition has given us a massive range and choice of alphabets. There are well over 10,000 current styles of alphabet based on Roman lettering, all of which, excluding the German Blackletter, can be said to be derived from six basic alphabet families: old face, modern, transitional, Egyptian, old style and san serif. There are a number of terms used to describe these type styles. They are illustrated on page 11 as examples demonstrating the differences between them, not as recommendations for their use in signing. Contemporary typeface design has to some extent blurred the boundaries between these traditional categories.

Suitability for signing

There are arguments to suggest that certain alphabets are particularly suitable for signing purposes. Certainly some are more legible than others but this does not make them better in all circumstances. Nor is it a reasonable argument that alphabets that have been derived from buildings – the Roman serifed capitals, the Sans, the English signpainters slab-serifed Egyptian or the Arabic Kufic style – should be adopted.

The reasons for such a number of printing types were primarily function and fashion. Certain cuts of letters were found to be suitable for different printing processes, or different paper, some being particularly legible and easily read in blocks, others confined to display. Individual preferences and tastes have also had their influence.

Every western typeface alphabet is comprised of two distinct and different alphabets: capital letters and lowercase letters. At one time, italic, a cursive form of the Italian hand, was an independent rival to the Roman typefount, but the more usual forms of italic today are inclined. Alphabets used in signing may have Roman and italic versions and a variety of sizes, weights and decorative styles – for example, shadows. Words from a single alphabet can thus be given quite different appearances and visual associations.

The history of signs

The history of signs has enjoyed an amount of scholarly study and practical investigation. The historical development of individual sign types, including inn and street signs, has been particularly examined. Unfortunately a history of all signs does not exist and would be almost impossible to cover in its entirety.

Architectural lettering

It is worth making the distinction between general signs and architectural lettering, which is lettering that has been designed as an integral part of buildings or structures. The history of architectural lettering is quite different from that of signs. Alan Bartram, in his book *Lettering in Architecture*, identifies the four main periods in which architectural lettering has assumed importance: in Roman times, during the Renaissance and Baroque periods, in eighteenth- and nineteenth-century England, and in Fascist Italy. But as Nicolete Gray so clearly indicates in her classic text, *Lettering on Buildings*, 'For us, unfortunately, the architectural letter is neither living as a tradition nor collected as historical material. One can only make fragmentary notes.'

The study of signs

Signs originated and developed with the need to communicate information. Hanging signs are among the oldest forms of advertising, dating back to Roman trade and guild signs. At Pompeii, such examples can still be seen, together with election signs painted on the walls. Many of today's signs and symbols were conceived in medieval times, and in the sixteenth and seventeenth centuries. With the rapid expansion

of handicrafts and commerce during the seventeenth century, the number of labelling or identificational signs multiplied. Badges in the form of familiar objects were easily pictorialized, and these pictograms were often modelled in three dimensions and used as identification.

This system was later adopted by proprietors of service industries, such as banks. As the need grew to communicate to the expanding population, clear, effective and often beautiful signs were developed. In the eighteenth century hanging signs were the standard practice. Gradually, names came to be painted on window sills and walls. Fascia boards are a comparatively recent arrival, perhaps a solution to the restrictions imposed on hanging signs, and perhaps also due to Victorian status consciousness – a personalized fascia board was distinctly more impressive than an impersonal hanging object. In the nineteenth century, street numbers also made their appearance.

As transportation and communication routes became more complex, signs were increasingly used for identificational and directional purposes. Today it would be impossible to navigate any unfamiliar road system or international airport unaided.

▲ London-based Lloyd Northover Design Consultants designed this sign system for Schreiber Furniture. Their highly legible signs are an impressive vehicle for the company's visual identity.

▶ This exciting piece of environmental lettering by Chermayeff and Geismar, in New York, has a timeless quality. The stove-enamelled identificational '9' looks splendid on this Manhattan street.

IN CASE OF
FIRE
USE STAIRS
UNLESS
OTHERWISE
INSTRUCTED

NO SMOKING

ELEVATOR
BANK

S

YOU ARE HERE ▶

Signs are an integral and essential part of our environment, necessary for the effective and safe use of all transportational facilities, the promotion of business and the communication of knowledge and ideas.

Sign categories

Signs loosely subdivide into six main categories or sign types: orientational, informational, directional, identificational, statutory (regulatory) and ornamental. However, it is impossible to categorize signs in an absolute fashion, and part of their fascination and interest is that they fall within many areas and their meanings may be interpreted on different levels. Indeed, some of the most interesting and beautiful signs serve a largely decorative function.

Orientational

Orientational signs locate users in an environment. Such signs include maps, exploded views and plans at entry and decision points, architectural reference points and landmarks.

Informational

Most lettering may legitimately be described as informational. While catalogues, timetables and directories all contain information in book form, informational signs are everywhere in the environment. Such information may concern opening hours, merchandise, forthcoming events and so on. The form of the sign varies enormously with the information being communicated.

▲ This elevator-call button plate fits over the smaller plate supplied by the elevator manufacturer, and can be removed for servicing. In this way Vignelli Associates have incorporated the obligatory New York City information regarding egress during a fire.

▶ This delightful piece of signwriting for H.J. Glew identifies a local builder in a small Cambridgeshire village in England. The lettering is strong and functional, and implies that H.J. Glew is a builder who can be trusted.

Informational directories are vehicles for listing large amounts of information. They are used in many different contexts, such as restaurants, reception areas and retail stores. Provided that they are comprehensive and well placed, at major entrances and decision points, they help to reduce confusion and enquiries to staff. Instructional signs tell people what, or what not, to do; these tend to be kept separate from all other signs.

◄ This beautiful calligraphic name, applied to glass, is a very simple way of identifying a personal space. It is both elegant and effective.

► The New York Vietnam Veterans Memorial, designed by Peter Wormser, William Fellows and Keith Helmetag, is a structure devoted almost exclusively to words – the dialogue between Veterans and their families. Etched in glass, it vividly and movingly evokes an era.

Directional

Directional signs are explicit navigational tools. They are usually part of a sign system, whether it is a motorway system or a series of signs within a contained environment such as a sports stadium or an office complex. Sign systems in high-stress environments, including airports and hospitals, are essential for their safe and efficient use and provide valuable reassurance for users. Good directional signing is becoming more important in the UK, with its increasingly congested road system.

Identificational

Identificational signs are essentially labelling devices which confirm destinations or establish recognition of a particular location. Signs may label a work of art, a structure, a building or group of buildings and environments. This traditional form of identification usually denotes ownership of some kind and these signs tend to be 'one-off' or individual. Identificational signs may be used to advertise a business or activity, such as the local pub or high-street shop. Larger companies use consistent, mass-produced signs as part of corporate identity programmes. Internal identificational signs help in the location of items, whether it is in the local supermarket or a museum. Individuals also like to personalize their property through identificational signs.

Statutory (regulatory)

Statutory signs display rules-of-order, as for conduct or prohibited activity, prescribed by local regulations, owners or other authorities.

They exist mainly to safeguard and protect people against danger. Such signs are mandatory on dangerous chemicals, machinery, public buildings and various forms of transportation. Signs in this category include legal notices, security regulations, traffic control devices and markings and exit signs. They also inform people about procedures in the event of emergencies such as fire, sinking of ships, earthquakes and so on.

In the early 1990s the debate about signing in relation to emergency situations is of increasing concern. Signing was discussed following the fire disaster at Kings Cross underground station in London. It has also been suggested that the lack of clear signing at Hillsborough Stadium, where ninety-five football fans were crushed to death, may have contributed to the tragedy. Little is actually known about the behaviour of people when confronted with emergency situations, and as yet there is an insufficient amount of research on which to base important design decisions.

Ornamental

Ornamental signs embellish, enhance or beautify the appearance or general effect of an environment or its individual elements. Such signs include banners, flags, fences, tablets, commemorative plaques.

◀ Building the OXO letters into this factory tower on London's South Bank indicates company pride and commitment; blue ceramic tiles spell out the product name. It is a permanent advertisement as well as a favourite city landmark. Work is currently underway to restore the tower and its lettering to its former glory.

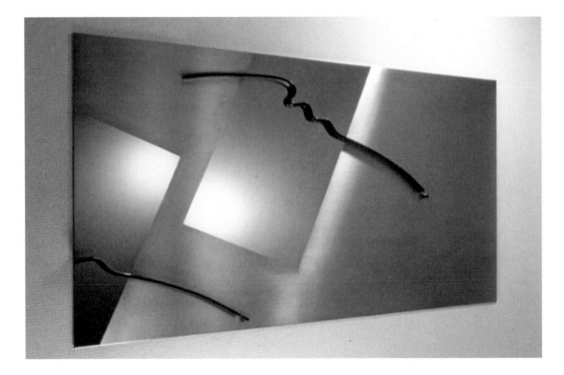

▲ Douglas Doolittle designed this visual identity for the Hotel de Mikuni, which he describes as 'aesthetic, ageless and everflowing throughout all the applications.' These stunning signs are made of brushed mirror stainless steel.

◀ Mikuni is a French chef of international standing who is known for his great artistic detail. His widely acclaimed restaurant in Shinjuku-ku, Tokyo, required a creative identity which reflected such stature.

Corporate identity

The most noticeable of all signs are usually those which form part of a commercial corporate identity. The term 'corporate identity' can mean different things to different people; it is an American term which is more or less synonymous with the English 'house style'. To avoid any confusion, it is here taken to describe 'the outward manifestations of an organisation and its activities – as perceived by its target publics and the public at large. It is the cumulative effect of these manifestations, over a period of time, that helps people to identify a particular organisation, corporation, company, institution, authority, association, etc, against its manifold background' (Dr R.H. Beck, 1971).

Corporate identity is a holistic term; it is contributed to by personal contact, impersonal contact through verbal communication, direct or hearsay experience with the company's product and services, its manner of doing business, the behaviour of

▲ Commercials director Simon Delany asked Smith and Milton for a classic underivative visual identity for his new London film company formed with Carrie Hart. Jemery Tilston designed the type, which was carved in slate by master craftsman Richard Kindersley.

◄ Pentagram's colour-coded fabric banner signing for the V&A Museum in London is simple and it works. It is accompanied by a new guide to the Museum, sponsored by Mobil, which incorporates the new colour scheme.

► This is a striking example of a building almost obliterated by advertising. Hong Kong, one of the world's most successful capitalist economies, seems here unwilling to draw the line between architecture and advertising.

its personnel, its size, age, structure, the nature of the activity, company history and success and corporate visibility.

The importance of a visual identity for many companies is no longer an issue, it is an accepted fact. It helps create an easily recognizable and distinctive public image necessary for a company's survival and growth in a competitive market. For a company in the services sector the design of the visual identity in all aspects becomes crucial, as it is the only face it has to present to the customer. Signs play an essential and increasing part in the advertising and visual-identity programmes of many companies, corporations and organisations. Visual identity as it relates to signs may include the corporate name, logotype, emblem or symbol and house colours.

Corporate-identity signing programmes are also about attitudes and self esteem, just as important within a company as outside. Consistent, well-designed signing, from doorplates to building identification, is an outward manifestation of internal efficiency and commitment. Employees get a feeling of belonging to an organization that is caring and secure. On a large scale, designing signing systems can be more problematic, because of the implementation and management, than other areas of design, with its specific problems of constant change and maintenance, but the rewards are multiple. A prime example of company pride and commitment is the 'OXO' tower on the south bank of the Thames, in London.

No one can accurately estimate the actual importance of a corporate signing programme, but what is evident is that an organization with clear, consistent and well-applied signing will be viewed in a more positive light by its customers and employees than one without such provision.

Issues

Visual-identity schemes raise many issues: a company is perceived through its physical representation, marketing, architectural and environmental compatibility, advertising and so on. A visual identity communicates a desired image, and according to Sandy Belford, head of corporate communications at Allied International Designers, it is also '[by] means of consistency, about controlling people's understanding of a company'.

Signs and architecture

A debate which has received much design-press attention concerns the relationship between signs and buildings. Buildings should be intelligible; one which is inwardly or outwardly confusing is simply badly designed. However, as buildings grow in complexity, the need for good signs becomes obvious; without them people become disoriented and lost. Ideally signs should complement the architecture. There are some exquisite examples, including, for instance, Pentagram's new signing for the Victoria & Albert Museum in London, designed by Alan Fletcher. The compass-point colour system of the elegant fabric banners do not compete with the architecture, and 'paradoxically it has the air of a temporary exhibition about it,' suggestive of a 'special occasion' (Hugh Pearman, 1989).

Naturally enough such consideration is not given to commercial high-street or downtown signing, and in both the UK and the US, people have become aware of the visual deterioration of these environments. Martin Pawley, architecture correspondent for *The Guardian*, passionately argues the case for a reassessment of the changing relationship between signs and buildings. He sees our contemporary environment 'besieged by a cacophony of words, signs and images, each directing, shouting and cajoling...' Despite increasing concern with environmental pollution, Pawley suggests, we are seemingly oblivious to visual pollution – the proliferation of signs. Often the clearest visible indicators of our continuing exploitation of the environment, and usually the result of short-term commercial thinking, signs have become 'disposable communication for a throw-away culture'.

Are the number and poor quality of many signs desensitizing people to their environment? If this is so, do designers have a responsibility that can be realistically exercised? As communicators, should designers concern themselves with the broader context: how signs operate within

◀ Chermayeff and Geismar temporarily transformed this Boston financial centre, for Rose Associates, by designing winter holiday displays, installed using thermo mylar. The six-storey atrium building, viewable from route 95, became the sign.

▶ This magnificent sign sculpture, designed by Chermayeff and Geismar, is based on the Mobil corporate 'O' symbol. The helix form was derived from the operations task of the New Jersey facility identified by the sculpture. A creative addition to the rural environment.

◄ This wonderful construction barrier, designed by Vignelli Associates for 712 Fifth Avenue, New York, is a life size blueprint of the building restoration to come, and won a 1988 SEGD Honor Award.

► Signs can be fun. In Zurich, Switzerland, bicyling sausages announce a bicycle race that passes through the town along this route. What a wonderful idea.

the structure of society, how they manipulate and are manipulated? The designer has a responsibility to the client, the user and the environment. Indeed, Michael Glickman suggests that the designer 'should be the mediator between man and his manufactured objects, systems and environment... a role of awesome responsibilities and great rewards'.

Retail

Nowhere is the temporary nature of design more of an issue than in retailing, with the recent phenomenon of the rapidly decreasing lifespan of retail identities. Some companies 're-fit' complete stores virtually every year, adopting a new visual identity. Signs, made of temporary materials, exist as part of the interior wallpaper that hangs on image-free architecture. Are designers making a valuable contribution to the environment, or merely providing a service for the client? Some would argue that the skills of a designer should aspire to permanence; others, that retail is a

dynamic discipline, more in the line of fashion, and that designers should be setting the pace of change.

Advertising

The issue of advertising signs in the promotion of products, services and identities is one which has received much attention in the late 1980s. Should architecture be allowed to act as the billboard for advertising, or in some cases be obliterated by it? Or can a building or structure successfully 'become' a sign and make a positive contribution to the environment, like the winter displays for Rose Associates by Chermayeff & Geismar Associates of New York? A further interesting development in advertising is the inclusion of photographs of 3-D signs in a company's promotional literature.

Signs today

Signs are environmental details, but they are essential to our understanding of our increasingly complex built environments and important because on the whole they are permanent and imposed. Unlike television or the printed word, they force us to look at them precisely because they are part of the fabric of the environment, and as such can take on a life of their own. Many older signs create beautiful effects through chance and time: bits fall off, are faded, reflected, cast interesting shadows, become distorted, folded, twisted and so on. Signs designed today provide an opportunity for improving and embellishing the environment deliberately and creatively. Some signs have a limited lifespan; others will last for years and be enjoyed by generations.

Signs are also subtle indicators of attitudes and change within society. 'If a society cares about trivialities such as either saving or creating a fine piece of lettering, it will probably care about the building it is on, and care about the street that it is in, and care about the country itself' (Alan Bartram, 1975).

In his book *Learning from Las Vegas*, Robert Venturi suggested that modern architects have 'abandoned a tradition of iconology in which painting, sculpture and graphics were combined with architecture'. The new 'humanistic' architecture of the late twentieth century has seen a general movement towards the reintroduction of ornament, and signs are part of that movement.

Theo Crosby of Pentagram suggests that part of the new direction in architecture is a massive concern for history, and for the systems of thought and forms that once made buildings responsive to their users. He argues that a methodology of ornament has become essential, but is not easily found in the artists and craftspeople of the past few decades as their work tends to be unrelated to building. 'To pull together the cultural strands into a new synthesis is now a great, necessary but very difficult task. It is the creation of a new poetry of place.'

Case study:

▲ **For the Pier 17 Pavillion in New York, BTA scaled the lettering for legibility from the Brooklyn shore and from boat traffic. The sign is also very successful from close quarters.**

Signs may be employed to help create a 'poetry of place'. They may also be used as a technique to link buildings and spaces together visually. South Street Seaport, in New York City, is a fabulous example of the revitalization of part of the long-neglected waterfront, in which signs have played a major role.

The environmental graphic design brief for Benjamin Thompson Associates (BTA) was wide-ranging: overall identification of the South Street Seaport Museum, logos for the two new buildings (Fulton Market and Pier 17) and signs for some public and interior spaces as well as for two hundred individual shops and stalls. In fact, BTA opted for tenant participation in the design of the shop and stall signs, within design and materials guidelines.

The main goal was to enable users to find their way around the environment without it being dominated by the graphics. The designers used 'clean and dignified lettering – Times Roman and Bodoni – and exposed metal fasteners, standard angles and metal panels [which] responded to the nature of the buildings, which were designed with exposed steel frames and other "industrial" details' (Jane Thompson, 1985). The spirit of the place is extended through the details of the signing. As a counterpoint to the BTA signs the tenants were encouraged to explore individual flamboyant options.

South Street Seaport

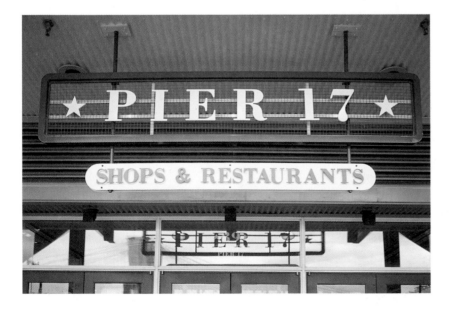

▲ This is the main identificational entrance sign, showing the detail of the cut-out metal letters against an industrial metal grid, within a strong visual frame. The 'Shops and Restaurants' panel hanging underneath is a solid counterpoint to the main element of the sign.

◀ This cold-cathode treatment of the Bluefish logo is one of the many fun signs within the Pier 17 scheme. The diversity of materials offers visual variety, while the consistency of the logo reinforces the theme.

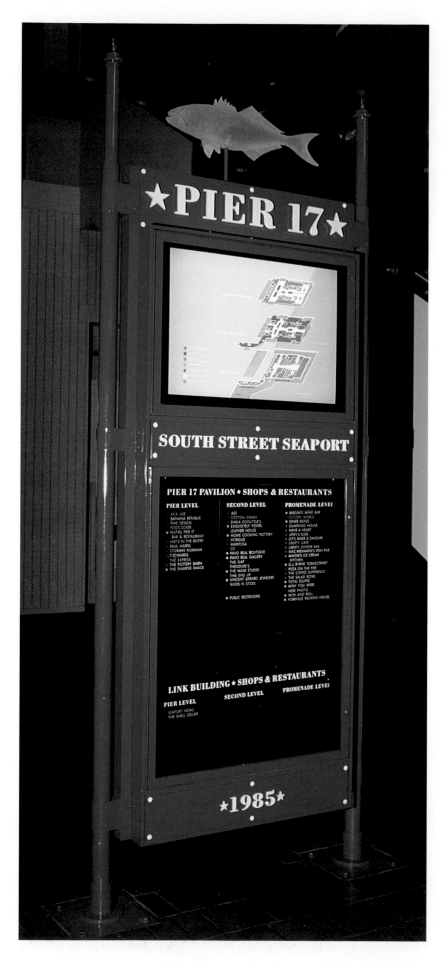

◀ This changeable site directory is topped with the Bluefish logo. The extreme clarity of the sign is due to the strong contrast of white lettering against a deep-coloured background.

▶ A close-up of the neon fish shows the attention to detail of the drawing within the lighting tubes.

▶ The Bluefish logo, this time in a gold version, is used as an easily recognisable way of making signs stand out from their environment.

The integration of graphics and architecture was central to the re-creation of the spirit or 'genius loci' of the place. The logo for Fulton Market is hand-carved in granite slabs that combine to form a wall cap, encompassing the building and marking each opening and pediment. A single display of cut-out metal letters with a white enamel finish marks the principal corner and harmonizes with the metal canopy from which it hangs. The Pier 17 Pavilion is lettered on its two sides. The size of the letters makes it visible from the Brooklyn shoreline and passing boats in true nineteenth-century style.

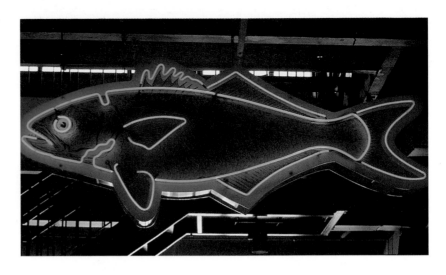

The Bluefish is the Seaport logo, and it has been described in a variety of materials for building directories and identificational and illuminated signs in both buildings. The palette of materials for the whole project is designed to respond to the aesthetic of the buildings, and recalls the metal, porcelain and painted signs indigenous to the history of the area.

South Street Seaport is extremely successful: attention to detail has provided New York with one of its most popular environments.

▼ This splendid moving sculpture by Hiroshi Yoshioka for Seibu Yurakucho in Tokyo is a magnificent display of colour, light and form. He writes, 'the straight line-up of figures impressed me so much with the sound of the word and its form, both independent from each other.'

1   The design process

1

The design process

▶ This design Victoria Wine Company UK by Design House uses colourful and humorous graphics to represent the products being sold. The mosaic lettering in the entrance conveys a traditional approach.

Each signing project is a unique, multidimensional, interactive design process, and in view of the recent addition of signing to the designer's portfolio, it could be difficult for a designer to know where and how to start. This chapter in no way seeks to give all the answers, particularly where complex design problems are to be solved, but aims, as a constructive design reference guide, to describe each stage of the design process. The first stage is formulating the problem, which means clarifying, defining and limiting it. There are two main considerations: the people involved – the client and the designer – and the actual design project itself.

The client

A good relationship with the client is essential for the successful definition of the design problem and therefore its ultimate solution. The client is in an unenviable position when it comes to choosing a designer or a design group. Unlike architecture, there is no compulsory professional body or legal qualification to help distinguish the professional designer from the amateur. Nor are there specific publications listing designers who undertake signing work, and even general directories can be misleading. In this embryonic, imperfect market, the client faces a high-risk choice.

The client will want to know that the designer not only has flair, technical competence and experience, but also understands what is required and will deliver it on time and within budget. These judgements may be made very subjectively: on everything that is seen, on personal presentation and on attitude, for example. The client may also judge the designer's manner of expression,

the care taken to listen, to take notes and to ask appropriate questions.

Some clients may not have worked with designers before, and many will want to gain more from the relationship than simply a successful piece of design. When working with a creative design professional, they will expect a range of experiences, wanting to have fun and enjoy a taste of a somewhat overglamourized design world. They will want to feel involved with the project and be part of the design team. Indeed, recent years have shown an increasing trend towards less confrontation and more co-operation between clients and designers, building a mutually beneficial relationship. The client is a valuable part of the team, possessing the essential information to help define and solve the problem. It is also the client who will decide whether or not to implement the final design proposal. And a 'good' client may be a source of inspiration to the designer.

Each client and company is unique. It is always helpful for the designer to

have done some initial research before any client contact. If the client has little experience of design, it falls upon the designer to educate the client in the process. Both client and designer will need a secure working basis, where they can be honest with each other and where responsiblities can be clearly spelt out.

The benefits of a good client relationship are many, not the least being the likelihood of loyalty and return business. Over time, the designer may be consulted at an increasingly early stage in the life of a job, which can be a creatively liberating experience, as the earlier the designer is involved, the greater the number of creative options that can be considered:

'One of the truisms I've learned is that the graphic designer can never be brought into a project [too] early. Not only does ample design time help avoid having to "stick a sign" on the wall, but it enables us to more easily achieve integration of the signing with the architecture in terms of scale, material, colour, and composition' (Bruce Hopper of Bruce Hopper Design Inc, 1979). In an established client relationship the designer may even suggest new projects to the client.

The client will also want to be respected as the person who is footing the bill; the arrogance of certain designers would suggest the client in the role of patron, not employer.

The designer

There are four fundamental requirements of the designer: the motivation to solve the problem, openness to experience, accurate systems for evaluating the ideas, and the ability to play with components and concepts. When presenting designs to the client, the designer is expected to be lucid and logical, showing an understanding of the problems, the business, and the operational environment. Communication can sometimes be a problem, due in part to the nature of the language of design; it will improve, however, if the designer is visually and verbally sympathetic to the client's 'language'. This will normally focus the attention on defining and solving the design problem.

Whilst formulating the design problem, designers often complain about the difficulty of obtaining information. The client can be the worst offender, and may need to be persuaded that the professional designer will respect client confidentiality and should have access to all the relevant material. The designer may also find information on signing difficult to track down. Sign manufacturers are gradually improving their promotional and technical literature, however, and trade magazines can be helpful. A trade reference bureau which includes sign and sign-related associations, companies, products, three-dimensional lettering samples and a list of specialized lettering artists and craftsmen is invaluable.

◄ Correct choice of material is fundamental to design of signs. This purple perspex sign in Bangkok, with white lettering applied on each side, cannot be read in sunlight, due to the show-through of the letters.

▼ ► Kenneth Carbone, of Carbone Smolan Associates, was the designer for the signs in the Los Angeles County Museum of Modern Art, California. Here, the lettering is in a legible sans serif face. The same company won the prestigious project to supply the sign system for the Grand Louvre in Paris. The informational and directional sign, below, successfully uses a combination of clear and discreet symbols to integrate into the classical environment of the palace.

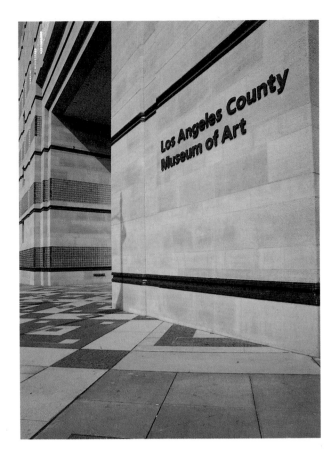

Naturally the designer should be honest about the amount of personal signing experience he or she has: after all, most designers have very little. If the job requires research time as well as design time, it should be built into the design proposal. As Jan Tschichold reminds us, 'Many signs and inscriptions have a long life. To rush the design of an inscription which will presumably be seen for ten or twenty years is wrong.'

The many limits or constraints of the job may have the effect of overloading the designer and putting a mental 'stop' on creativity. In the words of Richard Seymour, a partner in Seymour Powell, the London-based product consultancy, the designer may stay within a known 'operational envelope'. But a 'safe' design is a lost creative opportunity and personal creativity should continually be developed; it is the responsibility of the designer actively to seek creative development by constant exposure to fresh stimuli.

Initial client meeting
The initial or orientation meeting is the beginning of the designer-client dialogue, which ideally should have been preceded by an exchange of information. The designer should be presented with information on the background of the company, the nature of the existing signing and general design objectives for the new signing. The preparation and presentation of this information by the client involves and focuses their attention, exhibits a professional approach to business, and provides the basis for discussion and development. The information allows the designer to determine the scope of the design problem, although it may become evident that further research or information are required in order to define it more precisely. The client may need advice on how this can be done. This first meeting, as an introductory phase to the project, is the opportunity for the designer to ask the client to prepare the initial design 'brief'.

The brief
The brief is the statement, by the client, specifying the design requirements and the limitations imposed by time and money. There is no set format; its nature and detail are entirely unspecified. The brief is of fundamental importance and a 'point of opportunity' for the designer. In the words of Colin Porter, a partner in the London-based design consultancy Coley Porter Bell, 'A good brief encourages a good design solution.'

If the client is accustomed to working with designers, a brief may have been prepared in advance, and this will naturally form the basis of further

▲ Hiroshi Yoshioka, a retail designer, uses immensely strong three dimensional letterforms as the focus of this shop-window design for the Yurakucho Seibu Company.

▶ The Horniman at Hays project, in London, conceived and designed by Design House, is a tribute to Frederick Horniman, the Victorian tea merchant, traveller and collector. This beautifully worked brass floor plaque, intertwining the two H's, is a masterly detail in this rich environment.

► This lettering, running the length of a row of shops in Soho, London, is nearly indistinguishable due to the effect of cast shadows. The pots in the window above do, however, make it part of an interesting composition!

▼ The Rockefeller Centre, New York, is the prestigious setting for this piece of almost illegible lettering for the Boston Company. The letters are set forward on pins, casting this most unfortunate shadow.

discussion. If no brief has been prepared, the designer is in the fortunate position of being able to advise the client on the most helpful way to approach its preparation; the client should be decisive, honest, open-minded and creative. The brief should be as specific as possible about detailed, ordered design objectives, time and budget constraints, and payment procedures.

The design stage

The designer, now familiar with all the constraints of the job, can start to design the sign or sign system, or can in certain circumstances recommend an appropriate off-the-peg item to the client.

The design concept

The generation of each design concept or idea will be an individual exercise. Nicolete Gray suggests that the meaning of the words to be used on the sign may be the starting point. It could equally be the environment in which the sign is to be placed, or the interpretation of a mood, theme or message. If a concept eludes the designer there are a variety of techniques for the generation of ideas. Creative thinking techniques may be used to open the mind to applicable principles from the entire spectrum of experience.

Four ways to think laterally and solve creative problems – as advocated by the philosopher Edward de Bono:

■ To develop an awareness of the limitations of the way the mind works.

■ To develop the habit of using a quota of possibly three or four alternative ways of looking at a situation. The designer then proceeds along the most promising route. The imposition of an artificial quota gets the mind used to generating new ideas and approaches. Logical and mathematical techniques then refine the ideas.

■ To take the basic concept and change it round, by denial, turning it upside down, or reversing the relationships. This commonly used technique provokes ideas.

■ To use random stimulus. Inspiration can come from a dictionary or thesaurus. The systematic organization of words can provide valuable mind 'triggers'.

Reassessing the design situation, by summing up the problem in a short phrase or word and substituting alternatives, is another way of shifting one's viewpoint. A problem may be analysed by breaking it down so that the information is separated into easily manageable parts. These parts may be studied to see how they relate to each other. Additionally a designer may revert to the problem, or 'go back to square one' and take a new approach.

There are also exercises that require a number of participants. Brainstorming is a means of getting a large number of suggestions from a group of people in a short time. From these, possibly one or two sound ideas may be generated. Certain rules need to be followed; these four guidelines are the most important:

■ Participants should suspend judgement of other people's contributions; everything goes.

■ Participants should feel happy to free-wheel, to drift and dream around the problem.

■ The sheer number of ideas is important.

■ Cross-fertilization, building on the ideas of others, should be encouraged.

All the ideas are written down serially on paper and at the end of the session participants vote on the most promising proposal.

Initially the design concept is worked up by the designer, through thumbnail sketches and later through more finished drawings. A more complex problem may suggest the construction of a three-dimensional representation of the concept. At this stage problems may be highlighted which were not apparent in the two-dimensional form. Models are also good 'tools' or 'props' to explain the design concept to the client. People tend to understand three-dimensional form more easily than abstractions.

Concept development

Several areas may be considered by the designer as the design develops: copy wording, letterform, colour and material, size, position and ambient lighting. They are not mutually exclusive and their categorization merely enables convenient identification and discussion.

Copy wording

The wording of signs must be absolutely clear. The copy (the headlines and text) should be consistent, as short as possible, positive and unambiguous. Ideally, the style of the copy wording should match its prospective audience. Signs speak directly to a succession of individual viewers, and the copy wording should observe the usual social rules of politeness. For example, 'Please show your security pass' is preferable to 'All passes must be shown', which is also ambiguous, suggesting that people must show all the passes in their possession. Friendly, positive wording as part of the design approach will help to encourage the user to respond in a positive rather than a negative way. There are no rules about who should write the copy. It is likely to be the joint responsibility of the designer and the client. Where copy needs to be in more than one language, a good translator should be used and a specialized foreign-language typesetter may be required.

Abbreviations

As a general rule abbreviations are not used where signs are for the use of the general public. Abbreviations can cause confusion and even a feeling of alienation. However, they may be unavoidable, and sometimes even desirable where there are security considerations.

Punctuation

There is usually no punctuation on a sign, no underlinings, commas, full stops and so on. Information which requires punctuation in order to be understood should not be contained in the form of a sign. Signs need to be read and understood fairly quickly, and too much information on a sign

may cause associated problems, such as driver confusion leading to traffic congestion. The emphasis of a sign is implicit in all the design decisions, including the size of the lettering and its position on the sign, or the sign's location and visibility against its surroundings.

Letterform

There are very few typefaces that have been designed exclusively for signing purposes; most have been designed for printing text matter. There is no such thing as a good or bad letterform – letters are good or bad according to use. However, there are some general points in the selection of a letterform. A 'classic' serif or sanserif letterform, such as Times, Frutiger or Helvetica, is a 'safe' design choice. Using unusual or quirky letterforms may make recognition and identification difficult, as would any radical departure from the accepted norms. The letter combination of the word also needs to be considered. Even where the letterform has been well chosen, there may be one or two letters in the piece which look 'wrong' and ruin the whole composition.

▼ ► The signing system for the Museum of Modern Art in New York was designed by Kenneth Carbone to integrate with the architecture. The typography is legible in a clear sans serif face, used for the interior and the exterior of the building.

Legibility

Legibility means letterforms that can be seen and comprehended. Although the importance of legibility has been overstressed in recent years, it is vital in specific situations where speed of recognition is imperative, such as directories, signs directing the movement of traffic or people, exit, warning and safety signs. Legibility is a complex problem, and depends on many interrelated factors. Certain electronic signs, for instance, are illegible in direct sunlight, and even the shadows cast by individual fixed letters can render a piece of lettering almost completely unreadable. Generally, people pick out those things which are familiar, so familiar letterforms are more recognizable than unfamiliar ones.

Familiarity can itself be a complex problem, and is dependent on a number of factors, including the observer's age and education. Memory plays a big part, and as people become familiar with new forms, previously illegible letters are recognized and understood. When designing for legibility, other subjective factors, such as motivation and state of health, may also have to be considered. For example, lettering in a sheltered housing project for the elderly might be significantly different from lettering in a university housing scheme or a night-club.

Some good basic guidelines on legibility arise from consideration of typographic principles. General principles of letter recognition suggest that letters should be sufficiently different to avoid the possibility of one being mistaken for another. The eye must be able to register the image quickly. Hairline strokes cannot be seen from a distance and therefore reduce legibility. Counters, the shapes inside the letters, should be kept clear and open; a condensed letter is less legible than a wider one. The choice of weight – the thickness, contrast of strokes and the proportion between face and counter – is important.

Words are read and recognized by their overall shape and not by the shape of the letters. The top half of the word is more critical than the bottom. Consequently, lowercase letters, with their irregular and therefore more distinctive outlines, are preferable to capitals.

▼ This fun letterform embodies the energy and spirit of the can-can. It is absolutely appropriate for its retail function without being garish or displeasing. The designer has achieved a wonderful solution.

Space is as important as shape. The spacing between the letters (letterspacing) must appear to create a visually consistent rhythm of strokes and spaces. The space between the letters should be about the same area, whatever the shape. Unevenness in letterspacing will cause the eye to 'trip', resulting in a loss of legibility and visual irritation.

Wordspacing must strike a balance between being too narrow, so that the words run together, and too wide, so that the eye trips into the space between the words. Linespacing must also be considered. Where several lines are to be positioned, their visual emphasis should be horizontal; interlinear spacing should be sufficient to ensure this.

Sans serif faces tend to require greater line-spacing because of the visual monotony of the letterform. Furthermore serifs suggest a stronger baseline, which tends to prevent the eye jumping from one line to another. Generally, letters with short ascenders and descenders require greater line spacing.

There are three basic methods of arranging lines of lettering: lining up on the left (the most usual arrangement), centring, or lining up on the right. For signs belonging to sign systems the random layout of lines should be avoided as this requires sophisticated design decisions, and would be almost impossible to carry out without destroying the uniformity of the signs.

Additionally, elementary principles of layout provide a means of achieving visual emphasis and therefore importance for appropriate words, such as headings. Separation of headings by the addition of interlinear space, or emphasis by the use of the margin, is adequate provided the title line does not require more positive identification. Greater degrees of emphasis may be achieved through the use of capitals, weight and colour and of course size. Capitals are perhaps the most obvious and elegant choice.

All-round margin spacing also needs to be considered, particularly where words are produced on a panel of some kind. Generally it is better to have a greater margin along the base than at the head, since words look visually more satisfactory if they are slightly higher than centre. The left-hand margin should appear smaller than the right.

Expression through letterform

Jock Kinneir, a well-known British designer of signs and sign systems, suggests in his book *Words and Buildings* that 'By its interpretation of the subject, lettering communicates what it would be impossible to spell out.' Added to the letters themselves, the choice of letterform expresses the 'message'. Layers of meaning may be added to a sign. The message may be entirely informational, in which case the choice of letterform will probably be a classic, legible typeface. Alternatively, letterforms may express a concept, a mood, a corporate philosophy or even a subtle political statement. The strength of the subliminal message should not be underestimated; people respond to visual stimuli without intellectualizing the intention of the designer.

The inherent messages in letterforms are based in their history. Unfortunately, unlike typography which is well documented, letterforms used on signs are not well-collected or catalogued and thus it is not easy for the designer to become familiar with them. Additionally, it is dangerous for a designer to apply typographical knowledge only to the solving of complex signing problems. It is best

► This splendid sign literally spells out the meaning of the word through the choice of letterform and the arrangement of the letters themselves. The red square dot over the 'i' completes the sign. A valuable environmental gem.

for the designer to build up a working knowledge, and therefore a working scrapbook, of ideas and inspiration, of sign-lettering on, in and around diverse environments. Clearly this is quite different from keeping up with the typographical fads and fashions of the graphics industry.

Personal expression

Signing is usually a permanent affair, except in specific retail sectors, and is not generally the place for the designer to express personal taste. The designer should be aware of the levels of meaning represented by chosen letterforms, and of the dangers of the inappropriate use of 'favourite' typefaces without proper consideration. Where a particular style of lettering is required for a job, a specific lettering artist or designer can be commissioned.

Colour and material

Colour is another important aspect of the design of signs and is naturally indivisible from the properties of the chosen material. Nicolete Gray goes further and suggests that, 'We have a tendency to think that black and white are not colours. It is indeed the primary fault of almost all modern labels that they are designed *in vacuo*, as if they were not going to be made in material in the same sense as the bricks and mortar to which they will be attached, but were some sort of disembodied principle.'

Colour and fashion

Good colour sense is essential for the sophisticated professional designer, and evidence suggests that this cannot be taught. However, as graphic design becomes more cyclical in nature, designers have become more aware of 'seasonal' colourways, colour changes and colour predictions. Such trends can be followed easily. For the inexperienced designer, choice of colour can be restricted to simple, manageable and effective permutations.

Colour in signing and architectural lettering follows no discernible pattern, other than echoing other design disciplines. Past fashions in colour usage can be effective in expressing the atmosphere of a previous age. Today, colour is often used only for conspicuousness: 'If you can't make it good, make it big, if you can't make it big, make it red' (attributed to Paul Rand). But to use colour in this way only is a missed opportunity for the creative designer. Colour can fulfil many obligations.

◀ The sign designed by Design House for this flower boutique takes up the colours and shapes of the store's contents and fascia.

▶ The signs on these London church doors, spotted and photographed by Ken Garland, use colour in a bold, refreshing and eyecatching way. The life of the church is expressed by the vitality and style of the doors themselves.

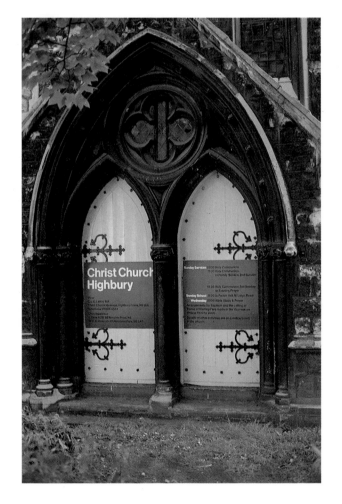

▲ This exquisite sign for Ficarazzi, in London, is subtly positioned on dark mirrored glass, which provides an appropriate degree of privacy within, and enhances the environment without by reflecting the splendid Antique shop opposite.

◄ Tilney Lumsden Shane have used a transparent, high-density plastic material for the external sign to the headquarters of the Financial and General Bank, in London's Belgravia. Its design enhances the bank's business profile and endorses its location in this Georgian conservation area.

► Ivan Chermayeff and Keith Helmetag designed the signs and the enamelled murals for this stunning pedestrian link between two subway lines in New York. The colourful approach to this environment is based on the subway colour-coding system and on the circulation patterns of visitors.

The functions of colour in signing

Colour can create an atmosphere: bright colours express excitement and fun, quiet colours dignity and repose. Colour can suggest unity or diversity; it can unite individual buildings that are different in scale, material or style. It can also be used as an informational and directional coding device, distinguishing one category of information from another. And finally, colour expresses the character of the material.

Colour defines form and may contribute to a sense of scale. In the same way that a building of one single colour canappear larger than a building divided by colour into smaller visual units, division of space may also be achieved through the colour and shapes of the lettering. The effect of tone and contrast creates the illusion of distance or close proximity. Alternatively, a transparent material like glass takes on the colour of its environment. Colour may also give a sense of weight; a black fascia board appears heavier than a white one.

Colour and symbolism

Additionally, colours have inherent symbolic meaning; in the past they have been adopted to represent ideas. Originally, the first relationship to be established was one of direct connection – if fire was red then red was a quality of fire. The second was dependent on the association of ideas – green, for example, was often associated with life. The third answers to arbitrary convention only, such as the use of amber for 'get ready' at traffic lights. A designer may need to be reminded of the established symbolic and cultural meanings of colour.

Size

The size of the lettering should be appropriate for the job which the sign has to do. Choice of size is largely dependent on the environment in which the sign is to be

placed. Increased size does not guarantee increased legibility, and size works in relation with other design decisions that have to be made, such as choice of letterfom and colour.

Large-scale lettering projects present very special problems. Such jobs are normally 'one-offs' and as such there can be few useful design guidelines. The size of the letters may be estimated by the use of scaled drawings and mock-ups. It is not uncommon for full-scale mock-ups of the lettering to be erected on site, enabling final design modifications before production. These mock-ups may be made from a variety of cheap materials such as expanded polystyrene.

With large-scale lettering it is crucial that the design is absolutely right. When successful it can be a wonderful, exciting addition to an environment, but a poor large-scale design is magnified by its size and is especially costly to put right. Large letters may need to be 'optically balanced' by the designer: this can be done by moderating the optical checks a type-designer imposes on letters which are to go through a reproductive process. The letter shapes should 'look' right. Large letters tend to require wider spacing than usual, and therefore more careful internal balance.

Positioning

The position of the lettering is very important; it must be correct in relation not only to the background but also to the people who are going to read it. When deciding on the correct position of the sign relative to the reader, basic physical factors should be taken into consideration. People generally see signs as part of the environment, unless they provide some needed information, and it is for the designer to decide how much a sign competes with its environment so that it is noticed and read. Signs must be positioned so that they are unobstructed within a person's normal field of vision and sight lines.

Normal field of vision.
A person's normal field or cone of vision covers an angle of about 60°. Areas outside this angle tend to be seen in much less detail. Whilst it is true that a person can enlarge their field of vision by moving their head, most people tend to resist this extra effort. For example, if a sign were supported from a high ceiling so that the sightline was more than 30° above eye level, it would probably not be seen. Consistency in the height of signs within a system increases the likelihood of the signs being noticed and provides a pleasing, uniform visual appearance that suggests organizational efficiency.

Background

In most graphic design the background is a page or a defined two-dimensional area. In signing, the background to a sign or a sign system is three-dimensional and may play a significant role in its design. The background may be a built environment or a rural environment, interior or exterior. The designer has to consider environmental factors such as air, space, light, movement and so on. In certain settings the designer may wish the signs to blend in with their surroundings. In areas of outstanding natural beauty, for example, the use of natural or transparent materials might be considered. Signs can either be free-standing or applied to existing structures. In the case of a single sign or individual letters applied to a building, the size and proportion of the building will form the immediate background or 'grid' within which the design works. The colours and textures of the surfaces all require consideration.

Background and legibility
It is normally essential that the background does not visually interfere with the reading of the letterforms. Letterforms should be visually isolated, so a plain, static background is usually recommended. Cut-out letterforms fixed directly to the background tend not to be as legible.

◀ Signs in Venice are often delightful, and this Alitalia sign is a striking example. Many directional mosaics are embedded in the streets around St Mark's Square. Their position enables them to be independent of any similar competing visual information, though they rely on relatively uncrowded pavements.

▲ Vignelli Associates won an SEGD Award of Excellence for this project in 1988. The rooftop sign for the International Design Center, New York, which identifies the entire project, is made of 32-foot high aluminium letters, enamelled bright red.

◄ The Conran Shop in London uses the grid of this spectacular glass wall to position the letters above the entrance. The composition is confident, elegant and balanced.

▼ This identificational sculpture for Talleyrand Office Park in New York, designed by Gottschalk and Ash International, is a series of eight 'T's with a colour gradation of green to blue to soften the sign against its surrounding landscape.

Ambient lighting

Ambient light in the environment is another crucial consideration. Lighting levels are quantifiable, but a good rule of thumb is to say that as ambient light levels decrease, the contrast between copy and sign backgrounds should increase. Generally this is achieved by using light copy on dark panels or backgrounds, or vice versa. Whenever possible, samples of the proposed colours should be tested where they are to be positioned.

Analysing the design solution

By the end of the design stage the designer will have developed a concept by making a series of design decisions. A design solution or a number of possible design solutions are arrived at. It is at this stage that the designer usually takes a step back and analyses the solution, confirming its suitability.

The designer needs to go back to the original brief and ask questions of the proposed solution. The following is a random checklist:

- Does it answer the brief?
- Has the problem been solved creatively?
- Has the idea been pushed to the limit?
- Is it visually pleasing?
- Is the information given the correct degree of visual emphasis?
- Is the copy written in a readable manner?
- Is it highly legible?
- Is it appropriate for the people who will see it?
- Does it promote the right image?
- Can it be easily manufactured?
- Is it to budget?
- Is anything missing?
- As a designer, are you proud of it?
- Does the idea break new ground?

The above exercise is also helpful in the preparation of the presentation of the design solution or solutions to the client. It may flag likely questions or concerns on the part of the client, giving the designer time to prepare a well-argued case.

The design proposal

The aim of the client presentation is to get agreement for the proposed design solution; it is very much part of the design process. The designer has to be absolutely clear on what is proposed and how it is to be communicated most effectively.

The content of the presentation is likely to follow the requirements specified in the brief: the design solution, its proposed cost and timing. The presentation itself should be designed and structured in a conventional way: an introduction, possibly outlining any research and conclusions drawn from it, the explanation of the proposed design solution with expected cost and time predictions, and a summary of the main points. The visual material should always complement the verbal message, and not the other way around.

The visual material needs to be carefully and appropriately selected. It may range from individual presentation packs, prepared drawings, flip charts, overhead transparencies, 35 mm slides and video presentations to three-dimensional models. Full responsibility for any equipment involved in the presentation should be that of the designer. Nothing impresses a client less than a display of technical incompetence. Additionally, the cost of the presentation should match the expectations of the client; a lavish approach may be viewed as a waste of money.

After the 'formal' presentation there is usually a period of time set aside for discussion. The designer or design team should be confident and able to answer any technical questions about the proposed solution. If an illuminated sign is proposed, for example, one member of the design team should understand the technical details, or be able to introduce someone who does. Clients may need reassurance, especially if working with designers is a new departure. It is always important to encourage client involvement and questions. The client should be completely happy with the design proposal before approving the work, either unconditionally or subject to agreed corrections.

▼ This small shop in Cambridge, England, has a distinctive fascia board. It is made quite beautiful by the dappled light which falls on it through the trees opposite.

Case study:

▲ A computerized system, such as the Apple Macintosh one being used here by Chermayeff and Geismar for JFK Airport, allows limitless, accurate, high-quality visuals to be produced. Design decisions can be quickly and effectively tested.

JFK 2000 is the largest airport signing project currently being designed in the United States (in 1990). The signing programme is being undertaken by Chermayeff and Geismar Associates in collaboration with architects Pei Cobb Freed and Partners, engineers TAMS Construction and SSVK, and the staff of the Port Authority of New York and New Jersey. The sign assignments include a comprehensive roadway programme, two parking garages, a new Central Terminal Complex (CTC) and a light rail people-mover, as well as a sign manual, construction graphics and an environmental art programme.

The project is interesting for many reasons. It is probably the most comprehensive co-ordinated signing programme ever to be designed. The dedicated design team estimates that it will take approximately two years to complete. The roadway package alone involves over 1000 signs and the sign construction budget will be a multimillion dollar figure.

One of the most fascinating aspects is the way the design process is being managed. All the work is being done on the Apple MacIntosh computer system using a variety of software: Adobe Illustrator, Quark Express, Excel and Filemaker. Design, design presentation, development, construction documents and client presentations all involve the computer.

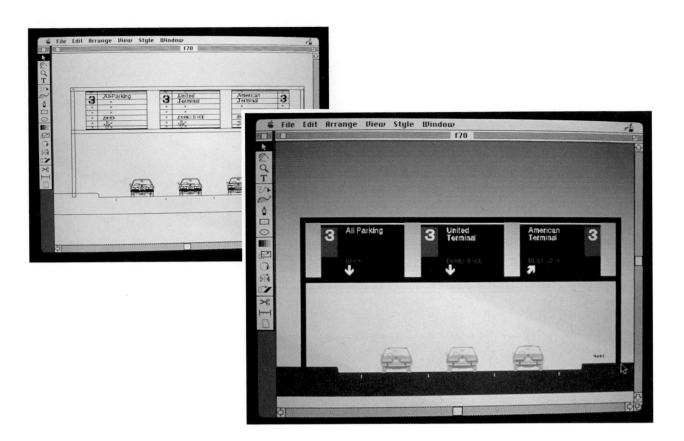

JFK 2000

▲ **Two stages of the same design: first showing grid lines without colour, and secondly as a coloured presentation drawing.**

▶ **This illustration of a computer screen shows the position and size of the lettering, the colours of the terminal designations and the red LED variable message display.**

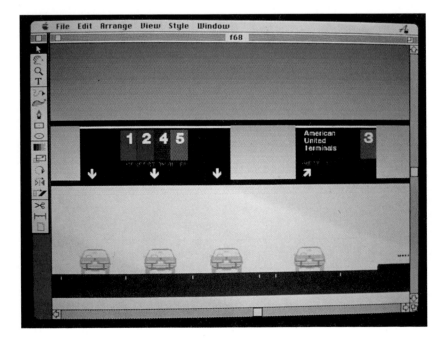

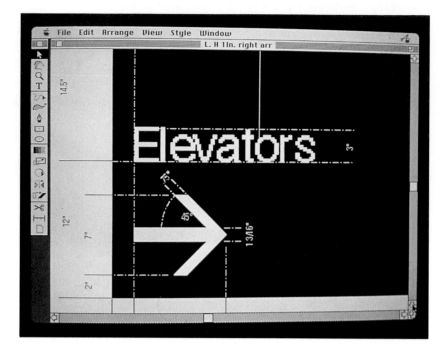

▼ The system allows working drawings to be completed on screen and produced as hard copy. Drawings are numbered and filed in a convenient way, with no fear of loss or deterioration in quality.

Chermayeff and Geismar has completed the design of the roadway signs for the first section of construction, and the principles developed are being applied to the remainder of the site. The signs employ a standardized grid lay-out which facilitates the positioning and size of all the lettering. Colours are used for the terminal designation. The majority of signs incorporate LED variable message displays delivering up-to-date information about traffic patterns around the airport, as well as parking availability.

The design for the signs in the CTC is at a schematic stage, and the role of the designers, to date, has been limited to researching the available technologies.

Detail of Neon Signage

Exit ⬆ خروج

▼ ▲ ▼ Here are some examples of the extreme accuracy that is possible using this system. Another advantage is the speed with which changes can be made and applied to the design of all or part of the scheme.

Chermayeff and Geismar is convinced that in the spirit of air travel in the 1990s, the use of a video-grid wall is appropriate for transmitting generalized information about New York City to visitors. It is expected that LED variable message signs will play an important role in the distribution of baggage claim and changeable information, and interactive video will be combined with vocal directions and hard-copy print-outs, to assist individuals in their wayfinding efforts.

This project is significant in its analysis of complex design problems and proposed solutions. When completed, it may well set a new standard for wayfinding in large transportational environments.

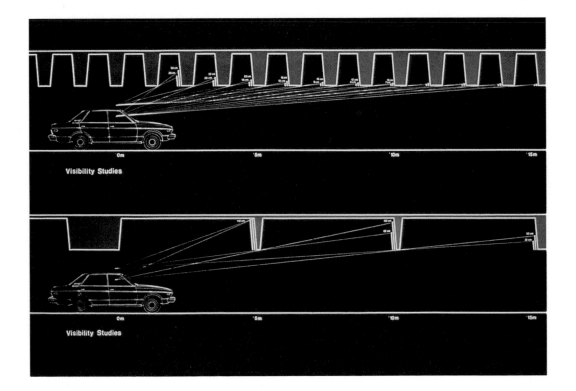

Visibility Studies

Visibility Studies

2 Project planning & implementation

Conran Design Group have clearly identified the lift lobby area at Gatwick North Terminal, with these large silhouetted letters, with their eyecatching blue illumination.

2

Project planning & implementation

▶ The brief to Fitch and Company for this out-of-town children's store was to convey the Boot's philosophy of care and quality and project the vitality and spirit of childhood. The brightly coloured totem logo, reminiscent of children's building blocks has been used in various three-dimensional forms both inside and outside the store and in a two-dimensional form on graphics.

Once the design proposal has been been accepted by the client, project planning and implementation can begin. The process may be simple for an individual designer working on a small job for a single-person client. However, it is likely to be more involved for a designer or design group working on more complex problems with larger clients. Decisions on who will do what, and how it is to be programmed, are crucial to the design solution being produced on time and to budget. Planning is a prerequisite for the successful coordination and implementation of a design. Additionally, a plan may be designed to be flexible, to incorporate agreed alterations with the client such as colour, letterstyle or material specification. Project planning and implementation may be subdivided into five categories: detailed design considerations, production and manufacture, installation, maintenance, and feedback and project evaluation.

Detailed design considerations

Detailed design considerations refine the design proposal, with the aim of resolving any design problems. The process includes consideration of legislation applying to signs, as well as the practical and financial management of the project. There are also, naturally, specific design considerations to be encountered when planning a large sign system.

Legislation

Legislation provides constraints within which designers must work, ranging from standards and codes of practice to guidelines and recommendations. Such standards may govern factors of safety, utility or appearance. Legislative constraints are inflexible and absolute. In architecture, such restrictions are usual; in mainstream graphic design they rarely apply. In the area of signing there is an immense amount of debate; the legislation is continually being updated as the whole area of signing develops.

UK legislation

In the UK there are three main areas effected by legislation: outdoor advertisement, health and safety, and fire regulations.

Outdoor advertising
Legislative consent is required for the display of an advertisement. This is usually obtained by the designer on behalf of the client. The definition of

◀ ▶ Trickett Associates, London, designed this statutory sign to work within the geometry of the chevron theme, right, for British Telecom Radiopaging. It also fits perfectly with the door detailing.

an advertisement is extremely wide:

...any word, letter, model, sign, placard, board, notice, device or representation, whether illuminated or not, in the nature of, and employed wholly or partly for the purposes of, advertisement, announcement or direction, [including] any boarding or similar structure used, or adapted for use, and for the display of advertisements.

Therefore the display of the legend 'Samuel Short, Family Butcher' on a shop fascia or a doorplate is considered an advertisement, as is a large product-advertising poster. In England and Wales, the local planning authority is generally responsible for the operation of the controls and for deciding whether or not a particular advertisement will be permitted.

Types of consent
Advertisements are divided into three groups depending on the type of consent required from the planning authority: advertisements which are excepted from the authority's control; advertisements for which the rules give 'deemed consent', so that the planning authority's specific consent is not needed; advertisements which require the

'express consent' of the planning authority.

For all practical purposes, most signs fall into the third category. Typical of this type are virtually all posters and illuminated signs, directional signs, advertisements on gable ends, and fascia signs on shop fronts or business premises where the top edge of the sign is more than 4.6 metres above ground level.

How to apply for consent
To obtain consent to erect an advertisement or sign, application must be made to the appropriate local authority (for the area in which the advertisement is intended to be displayed). Most authorities supply a standard form, which can be obtained from the local planning department. In addition to the completed application form, plans and drawings are required, together with the appropriate fee. Information on charges is given on the application forms, or can be obtained from the planning department's area office.

How an application is decided
Applications are usually decided by the council planning committee local to the site where the advertisement is to be displayed. Alternatively, the

planning committee may have delegated this responsibility to an officer of the council's planning department. In deciding on approval for the application, the planning authority may only consider two issues: the interests of amenity and public safety. Many planning authorities have formulated and adopted advertisement control policy statements, indicating the considerations they regard as relevant to their decisions. The designer might find this document helpful in preparing the application.

What happens after the decision
Consent for the display of the advertisement usually lasts for five years. However, the authority may grant consent for a longer or shorter period. Unless a condition is imposed that the advertisement must be removed after consent expires, it may continue to be displayed without any further application, although the authority may still take 'discontinuance action' against it.

How to appeal if consent is refused
If the planning authority refuses consent, imposes conditions which are not satisfactory to client or designer or fails to give a decision within two months of application, the right of

appeal may be made to the Secretary for the Environment, or, in Wales, to the Secretary of State. Appeals should be made within two months of the receipt of the notification of the planning authority's decision, although the Secretary of State has the discretion to allow a later appeal if circumstances are considered to justify it.

Health and safety
British Standard 5378 details the signing which is statutory for health and safety in places of work. The signs fall into four main categories, each with its own colour and symbol shape. The categories are: warning, prohibitory, mandatory and safe condition. The idea is that the symbol alone is sufficient to spell out the message, although sometimes supplementary words are needed. In the UK, safety signs complying with BS 5378 are available as stock items from specialist suppliers, who should also advise on current regulations and recommendations related to safety signs and products.

Fire
British Standard 5499 is an extension of 5378 and is concerned with fire. The Standard indicates the statutory signs and notices which identify fire-fighting equipment, explain the correct course of action in the event

of a fire, and show the safest way to evacuate a building. The local fire authority may have requirements which differ from or are additional to the British Standard. Equally, British Standards are regularly updated, so it is essential to check with the local authority for details of any additional recommendations or mandatory requirements. However, even if the British Standard recommendations have been exactly followed, the designer is not exonerated from any possible legal liability. The standards should be considered a minimum, and recommendations applied with care and thought.

European legislation
Other European countries have a similar approach to the public regulation of signs. The law generally provides clear, simple, environmentally sensitive standards for a case-by-case review of advertisements. Article 5 of the decree which applies French national advertising law to the Seine Prefecture states that 'Advertisements must not detract from the appearance of public places and private places open to the public.'

Similarly, Section 52 of the Building Regulations for Signs and Other Fixed Installations in Stockholm provides that 'Signs shall, as regards

shape, colour and design, meet reasonable requirements of neatness and suitability to the location. Particular care shall be taken that they do not have an injurious effect on the city or landscape appearance, or involve danger of fire or risk of accidents...'

US legislation

The legislation of signs in America is completely different from Europe. To understand this, it is necessary to look at the historic and legal precedents. Before zoning, US cities were built without control standards. Environmental, traffic and other problems resulted. In 1924 the US Supreme Court legalized zoning. As a result, cities today enjoy 'police powers', and the authority and obligation to protect property values and the right of enjoyment of property. Cities tried to regulate as little as possible and to be very precise so that the regulations or zoning ordinances were uniform throughout a city. Zoning districts resulted. 99.9 per cent of communities in the US have zoning. This reactive legislation has proved to be effective and has 'brought order out of chaos'. The problem, however, is that most ordinances are very complex and precise, leaving little to interpretation. Creative design solutions are

often outside the scope of the regulations. There is an increasing tendency for governmental agencies to over-regulate signs, to such an extent that designers may be commissioned not according to their talent, but on the basis of their ability to get approvals.

The magnitude of regulatory authority is vast. There are over 80,000 units of local and county government in the US, each typically enforcing their own individual sign ordinance. Each ordinance reflects the attitude of the local community towards signs and maintains definitions and terminology unique to their own documents.

The new comprehensive sign programme in Phoenix may suggest an answer to this national problem, encouraging designers to use their creative ability unrestricted by inappropriate legislation. In addition to public safety standards and electrical and structural requirements, the city of Phoenix now looks at aesthetics. By defining 'planned projects' the city can enter into negotiation and provide increased flexibility on signs where appropriate. The regulations respond to the needs of the planned environment without reverting to a set of categorical demands and have proved to be a way of enhancing the quality and effectiveness of signs in the city.

In fact there are also ways of working successfully within the existing system. According to SEGD members, relations between municipalities, real-estate developers and designers can be improved. The designer needs to take the responsibility of educating the others involved, starting the dialogue early in the project, making it clear that the design is something beneficial for the community, and expressing a positive attitude. Jan Lorenc of Jan Lorenc Design Inc, Atlanta, stresses that governing agents 'are often politicians who want to use their power base. Let them be part of the process. Don't overpower them.'

It usually makes a good impression to submit a polished, professional presentation to regulatory authorities. Designers should also be patient:

'With city agencies, things don't move ahead quickly. Dealing with bureaucracy takes a tremendous

▲ ◀ The sign system designed for the holiday company, Thomsons, by Trickett Associates uses images of escape to exotic sunny places - the signs themselves are spotlighted to enhance this effect.

amount of energy' (John Branigan of Edwin Schlossberg Design, New York, 1989).

Generally designers can increase their influence by becoming members of the Architectural or Design Review Boards (ARBs or DRBs). At present, according to Jeffry Corbin, 'Usually the review boards or sign code boards don't have a designer on board. You're lucky if you have a landscape architect: usually it's an engineer who doesn't give a damn how a sign looks.' Becoming involved is the answer. Terry Graboski of Beck and Graboski Design says, 'I do have an impact on the ARB. It's a small step, but the quality of the signs is improving. It's also an educational process for the architects and designers on the board. When a [signing] issue comes up, I'm considered to be the expert and I will deal with it.'

Managing the process

Management is a central part of the preparation of the detailed design proposal, which is presented to the client after the initial or outline

design proposal has been approved. People and financial management, and the particular problems encountered when planning a large sign system, all have to be considered.

People management

The designer, the client and the manufacturer are all vital to the success of the signing project, and possible communication difficulties exist between them all, in particular between designer and client. General comments have already been made, but there are also some positive, preventative steps which can be taken.

The roles and responsibilities of the people involved should be defined and fully understood by all. Extensive consultation should take place at all levels before and during the process. Communication is vital for success.

Ideally, one person from the client company should act as a liaison person. This person is in a key position, and should have responsibility for making decisions. The position should be fully supported by the top

management of the client company. In the US, this system already exists in some companies, typically major hotel chains, large developers and some authorities. The position of 'sign manager' is well paid, and the person is generally named as the 'client representative' in a job contract. The existence of such a person avoids any damaging internal client-company politics which would otherwise arise because of conflicts between different client members. Many designers have found it almost impossible to work with a large, unwieldy client representation or committee.

Vignelli Associates of New York quote the 'bureaucratic crudeness and a situation of unskilled management and labor [which] never could implement the program [for the New York subway signing] as well as was specified by a very accurate manual.' Vignelli describes the project as 'besieged with politics and inefficiencies. The operation was very successful, but the patient died.' He also comments on the 'tremendous discipline' required to implement and protect the mass transportation sign system, designed for the Washington Metro signing. Indeed,

▼ ▶ Pentagram were commissioned by the architects of Broadgate to design the directional signage in an extensive development for financial services organisations, close to London's Liverpool Street station. The signs were produced in two versions, freestanding solid bronze units (below) and wall-mounted sheet brass fixtures (right).

this is true for any sign system of a reasonable size.

Similarly the design team should nominate a team leader or client liaison person, who has primary responsibility for maintaining an open channel of communication with the client.

Financial management

Scheduling the work, costing the project, and presenting the cost estimate to the client are all crucial tasks at this stage of the project.

Scheduling

For a large signing project to be finished on time and to budget, it is necessary to establish a time schedule at the outset of the project. Time is often a critical factor: the client rarely allows sufficient time for the signs to be designed, and a system planned, manufactured and installed. One effective and simple method of scheduling work is a Gant chart, which organizes day to day tasks in a horizontal fashion. This system allows both sequential and concurrent tasks to be shown and facilitates estimation of the size of the team and the time required to complete the project. Calendar dates can be shown as target dates or deadlines, and meetings with the client or other involved parties may also be shown. For complicated projects, computer programmes are available for just this task.

Costing

A detailed spreadsheet for the project, covering all aspects of the work, is an invaluable tool for estimating and controlling costs, within an expected maximum. The costs of a project fall into three main categories: the design fee, the sign manufacture, and the installation and maintenance.

The design fee

All design groups have their own methods of costing, usually on a professional-fee-plus-expenses basis, consisting of the hourly charge-out or billed-out rate of the designers to the client, plus expenses. This is sometimes incorrectly referred to as the 'cost-plus' basis, a term which originated in US military contracts and refers to the cost of designing and building a product plus an agreed profit for the contractor. 'Expenses' is the term used for the cost of getting things done: materials, photography, artwork, typesetting, travel and so on. If signing is a developing area of business, the designer should be careful not to underestimate the actual number of hours required, especially on early projects.

Some clients may expect the design fee to be based on a percentage of the manufacturing or building costs, because of their experience with architects and interior designers. This is not recommended. Designers will find that the 'time worked' fee is a more reliable and honest source of

profit. A sign may take a long time to design, and yet be inexpensive to manufacture. Similarly the reverse may be true. Naturally the number of hours worked and by whom should be carefully monitored throughout the project. The designer will quickly gain experience and a 'feel' for cost implications.

The cost of manufacture, installation and maintenance

The designer must inform the client of the cost not only of manufacture or fabrication of the signs, but also of installation and maintenance. Often a number of estimates are obtained from different manufacturers. Installation and maintenance procedures are recommended by the designer, and the client and the manufacturer then agree costs. The manufacturer needs the following information to prepare an estimate: quantities of each item, shape and dimension, material and manufacturing method(s), copy application if separate and lighting requirements.

Obviously the more complete the information, the more accurate the estimate will be. An unusual or customized sign may be difficult to estimate. Depending on how many fabrication techniques are used, the designer may have to obtain costs from a number of specialists. Several days should be allowed for this process, and it may be wise to add a contingency of 10 per cent to cover unknowns. A time limit is usually

placed on the estimate by the manufacturer.

Value engineering

Value engineering, sometimes called 'value analysis', is an approach to cost reduction in which components are carefully studied to see whether they can be redesigned, altered, standardized or made by less expensive production methods. It is a useful design exercise which, ideally, should be employed for all custom-designed signs. The technique is more common in the US than in the UK. Unfortunately, it is usually used only on 'over budget' projects. The idea is to cut costs with no reduction in quality.

A value engineer examines the high-cost components in a sign, typically when 20 per cent of the components account for 80 per cent of the costs. A value engineer will also look for components that are over-designed, where their cost is disproportionate to their contribution to the overall concept. Deciding whether a component contributes value or not is often quite subjective. The designer has to decide where to stand firm and where to compromise: in aesthetic considerations the designer's word should be final. In structural considerations, designers sometimes have a tendency to 'play safe' and unneccesarily overbuild elements. In fact, structural elements can, and should, be accurately determined.

◄ For their new sign system for London Underground, Henrion, Ludlow and Schmidt made extensive use of the familiar roundel, here seen as an external identification sign. London Underground has over 280 stations, and the new scheme covers all signs for all stations - internal and external, identificational and directional.

A thorough breakdown of costs may reveal surprisingly expensive items or design features. These features are often assumed to be inexpensive because of their relative unimportance in the overall design. Occasionally, savings may be made by analysing broken-down costs with the manufacturer, if the manufacturer is willing to do this: most, however, are not. Features and sign details should always be considered in light of the final viewing distance. Most exterior signs are only ever closely viewed by the designer and manufacturer, where they are made. None the less there is never any excuse for poor workmanship; a badly made sign is not acceptable in any circumstances.

Sign manufacturers are seldom given ample time to bid for a project. Most signs are not 'value analysed' at all, they are costed very quickly by the manufacturer. Where possible, designers should develop good relationships with a variety of fabricators and select the most appropriate for the project. Such relationships will encourage a positive approach to the project, the discussion of budget considerations at an early stage, and the working together of designer and manufacturer as a creative team to solve problems.

The estimate of manufacturing cost needs to be accurate and carefully timed. If it is obtained too soon, insufficient information will be available to the manufacturer and the estimate will have little hope of being accurate; if too late the designer may not have sufficient time for design revisions. At this stage it is usually also appropriate to consider the cost of installation and maintenance.

The design presentation

Final designs can be presented to the client in many different forms, from scale models to perspective renderings, depending on the nature of the sign system, the preferences and expectations of the client, and the time and budget available. For most situations, elevations to scale, of major sign items, are presented with copy wording applied in a readable form. If the client is pleased with the presentation the budget may receive little attention. If there is a serious gap between what the client had in mind and a realistic price for the job, then the client may be willing to pay more, or ask the designer to value analyse the signs. Alternatively, the designer may be asked to consider the problem afresh, with price as a major constraint. However, if the budget is unrealistically low, a good design will be impossible to achieve.

One approach to the detailed project planning of a large sign system

Large sign systems often create specific organizational problems. This section discusses one approach to planning the process involved.

Initial survey

The designer is likely to be faced with one of two situations: signing a building or environment which is being designed or built, or signing an existing building or area which has inadequate signing or none at all.

If the building or project is still in the planning stage, the designer should try to be involved as early as possible in the programme, to maximize creative scope and ensure that the signs are considered part of the building contract and given due importance. Where possible, existing plans should be examined, and brought up to date if necessary. Many changes and additions to buildings and their spatial arrangements can take place over a period of time. Even small things such as occupants moving offices and desk layouts can be crucial to someone finding their way.

▼ Henrion, Ludlow and Schmidt undertook vast initial surveys in the course of their signing work for London Underground. Inconsistencies were found in the various sign types; this chart shows the location and frequency of the different sorts of roundels.

► ► The two examples of A4 record charts, overleaf, as used by the BDP design consultancy, show details of an existing four-language directory and a hospital room-numbering schedule, both useful for providing the context for future signing programmes.

●---Back-lit
●---Unlit

		Kennington	Embankment	Victoria	Leicester Square	Oxford Circus	Kings Cross St. Pancras	Baker Street	South Kensington	Mile End	Charing Cross	Heathrow Central	Hammersmith	Epping	Plaistow	Angel	High Street Kensington	South Ruislip	St. John's Wood	Arnos Grove	Farringdon
1	ON PLATFORM WALL Back illuminated on panel			Back-lit		Back-lit	Back-lit					Back-lit									
2	Back illuminated cut-out						Back-lit	Back-lit			Back-lit										
3	Vitreous enamel on panels			Unlit	Unlit	Unlit	Unlit		Unlit						Unlit						
4	Brass edged, vitreous enamel cut-out				Unlit	Unlit	Unlit	Unlit													
5	Convex surface							Unlit					Unlit			Unlit				Unlit	Unlit
6	3D, metal edged, vitreous enamel							Unlit					Unlit				Unlit			Unlit	
7	Brass edged, blue and white outline						Unlit										Unlit		Unlit		
8	Framed bar and outlined vitreous enamel circle	Unlit	Unlit		Unlit		Unlit		Unlit												
9	Laminated wall panels										Unlit										
10	Original 1906 solid disc and bar						Unlit														
11	Combined with line diagram												Unlit								
12	ON RAILSIDE WALL Vitreous enamel panel	Unlit	Unlit	Unlit	Unlit	Unlit	Unlit	Unlit	Unlit	Unlit	Unlit	Unlit				Unlit					
13	Laminated wall panel							Unlit			Unlit										
14	Brass edged vitreous enamel					Unlit	Unlit			Unlit									Unlit		
15	Vitreous enamel rectangular panel										Unlit										
16	ON PILLARS Vitreous enamel panel		Unlit							Unlit											
17	Brass edged vitreous enamel									Unlit											
18	Metal edged vitreous enamel												Unlit								
19	Screened panel												Unlit								
20	ON FRIEZE Contains name of line	Unlit	Unlit	Unlit	Unlit	Unlit	Unlit	Unlit	Unlit	Unlit	Unlit										Unlit
21	Roundel combined with trunking system			Unlit		Unlit	Unlit	Unlit			Unlit	Unlit									
22	Tiled						Unlit										Unlit		Unlit		

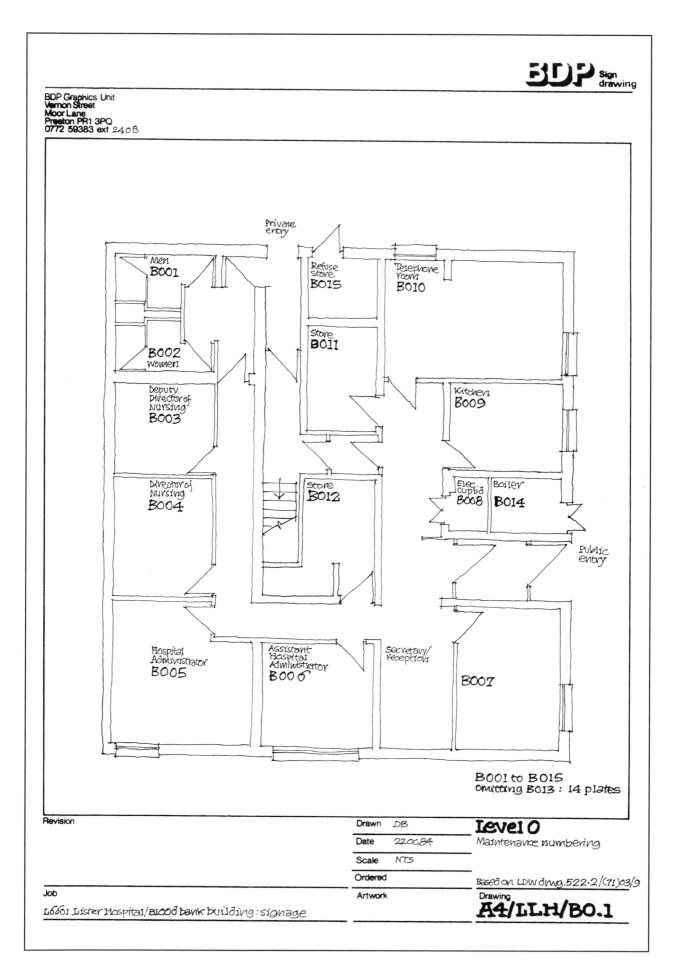

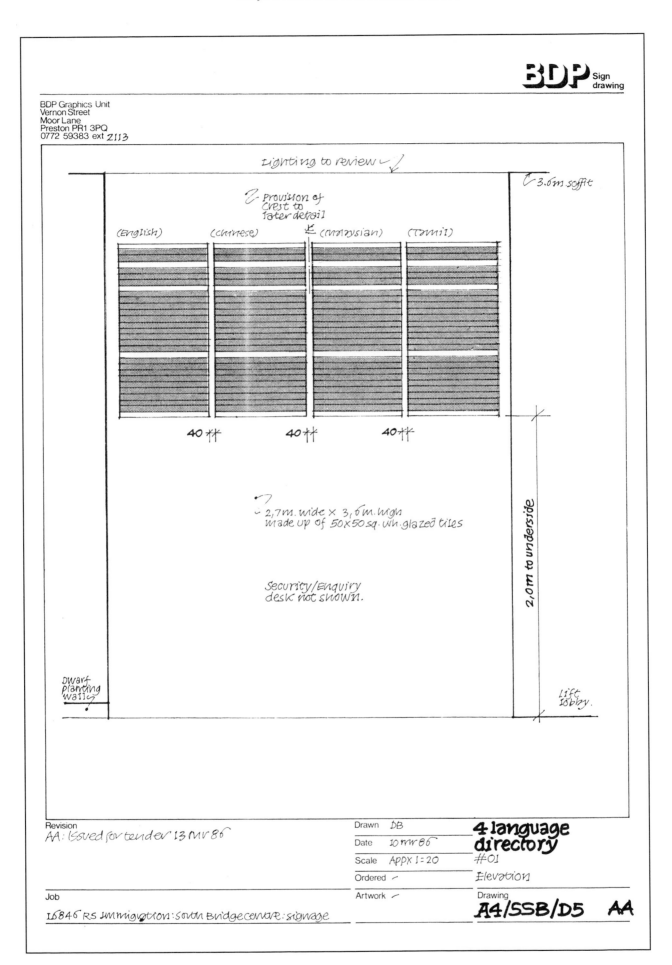

▼ Baggage reclaim area, Gatwick Airport, England. Conran Design Group designed these clear identificational numbers for this sometimes confusing and stressful environment.

For existing buildings, the initial survey should determine the patterns of building use. The designer is well-advised to visit the site straight away, whatever the size of the job. Photographs, as a record of the event and a reminder of the spatial arrangements and existing signs, are often invaluable, particularly if the site is a considerable distance from the designer's studio.

It is a good idea to identify the relevant spaces on the plan in a systematic way, and to mark the position of the existing signs using a number or letter system. BDP, a large UK multidisciplinary design consultancy which undertakes many signing projects, has an exemplary way of recording this information. All material (drawings and text), where possible is recorded on pre-printed A3 or A4 sheets as standard, so that this may be photocopied and distributed to all the many people concerned. As sign design normally involves the coordination and cooperation of a large number of people, including planning and fire authorities, the client, the manufacturer and so on, this can save the client administrative time and expense. Additionally, A3 and A4 sizes are convenient to handle when walking around the site, and A3 can easily be folded when filed with A4 pages. All recorded information is given a code number.

Who the users are and how they arrive

The identity, number and movement of users need to be established. It can be surprising just how many people use an environment. They each have a specific set of requirements to enable them to operate efficiently. The users may be categorized in the following way: permanent staff, temporary staff, members of the public, people making deliveries and collections, and members of the emergency services.

Permanent staff
The permanent staff are the normal users of the building. Most people quickly become familiar with a new

building layout, or indeed a new building. Very soon they begin to ignore signs in the spaces which they normally use. In view of this, it is essential that sufficient emphasis is placed on the statutory signs, such as fire exit and safety information, which need to be seen, read and understood immediately in an emergency situation.

Temporary staff

Depending on the number and frequency of use of temporary staff using the environment, certain additional information may be needed. Thought should be given to employment patterns, especially if they are cyclical in nature and if a lot of people simultaneously need to find their way around. A number of options may be considered: temporary signing or increased permanent signing are possibilities; in other circumstances, it may be better for temporary staff to be accompanied in unfamiliar environments.

Members of the public

Members of the public may or may not visit a building frequently. Again it is important to have as much information about these users as possible, in order to cater for their needs: how many, how often, at what time of day do they visit, and so on. Extremely clear signing is required. This is best achieved by considering a user who has no knowledge of the environment and makes no assumptions about its likely layout. Signs will then not only instruct but also reassure.

People with mobility handicaps and people with prams and pushchairs may require particular routes around an environment. These may be significantly different from the usual pedestrian routes, in order to avoid obstacles. The designer should also take account of the needs of individuals who are vision-impaired or illiterate.

Deliveries and collections

Deliveries and collections tend to take place in specific locations. These locations should be well identified from all approaches. Taxi pickup points should also be considered.

It is better to instruct people clearly than to allow them to get lost in an alien environment.

Emergency services

Police, fire and ambulance services have to identify locations in an emergency, at any hour of the day or night. Obviously the implications of a service being unable to do so are extremely serious, possibly resulting in loss of life. Conscientious signing will enable the services to act as efficiently as possible.

Having established some essential facts about the users, the next task is to determine how they arrive. The main methods of transport are on foot, by road vehicle, and by train. The building and entrance identificational signs should be clear, taking account not only of pedestrians who may approach the building from any direction, but also of drivers, who are likely to arrive at speed, needing to assimilate important information quickly and safely.

▲ Colourful hanging signs are visible from all directions for easy identification, with stylized images of the services and facilities available, suitable for the multi-lingual environment of Gatwick Airport. (Designed by Conran Design Group)

◄ The use of this creative, colourful illuminated signing helps set the mood of individual departments, and works in conjunction with the other lighting to give de Bijenkorf a warm, light, open impression: an inspired retail design.

► In this scheme for de Bijenkorf in Ultrecht, the Netherlands, Fitch RS have made the 'user path; into a directional tool. Together with a polished granite walkway, high-level cold-cathode bars illuminate the store and help customers find their way around.

▶ A statutory no-smoking sign designed with flair by Coco Raynes for University Park at MIT, Cambridge, Massachusetts. The choice of this green glass creates some interesting optical effects. The construction details are precise and neat.

Planning the signing system or 'scheme'

Most signing experts have a personal method for designing and planning the scheme, but all agree on the 'common sense' method of working from the general to the specific, starting with broad principles which cover all eventualities. Taking a general look at the problems and establishing these principles is important. All the available options should be considered at this point. For example, it may be preferable, where a client has a number of buildings, for the client to consider a change of building use, rather than sign a building which is busy and whose design does not fit the purpose.

When designing signs to fit an existing environment it is best to start with the building itself and look at its physical shape and location. Generally, the more complex the premises the more necessary an ordered and logical sign system becomes. Crucial considerations are the relationship with the environment, the main access routes to the building for all the users, and car-parking facilities. All existing buildings and rooms should be consistently identified. When looking at the problem as a whole, the designer may be able to suggest radical changes and improvements; in an extreme circumstance, for instance, it may be that a building needs completely new room numbering before the signs are even considered.

Working drawings

Working drawings explain the design to other designers, the client and the manufacturer. They include plans, elevations, sections and details of the signs. These drawings identify structure, material, colour, form, size, location and so on. Where mechanical or electronic devices are being drawn for fabrication, it may be that exploded views, isometrics or other types of flat and projected drawings are required to describe the components.

Plans

Scaled plans are an important device for the designer, and should be seen as aids to design. They enable the designer to see the whole scheme in the correct scale and proportion. This is an enormous help in establishing approximate visibility distances and the accurate positioning of signs.

The plans required for planning a signing scheme include:

■ A street plan, indicating the relationship of the building to the surrounding streets;

■ An exterior location plan, indicating external traffic circulation areas;

■ An interior location plan, indicating internal traffic circulation areas;

■ Floor plans, indicating each building floor.

If a self contained area is likely to have a number of signs, a further detailed plan may be useful.

The sign types required are best considered in turn: orientational, identificational, directional, informational and statutory and ornamental. However, these categories are not mutually exclusive.

Orientational

In unusual, complex or very large environments, orientational signs may be required to locate the user in the environment.

Identificational

These signs should readily identify the building or environment. Size and postion need to carefully considered. Once a proposed position has been established, an informal opinion may be obtained from the local planning authority. A common problem with large identificational signs is accessibility for cleaning and maintenance. Naturally, if the building itself is very distinctive, identifying signs may be almost superfluous; few people could mistake the Houses of Parliament, for instance.

Directional

For directional signs each 'user path' should be drawn schematically on the plans, and at each 'decision point' a sign should be positioned to indicate whether the user should go up, down, left, right or straight on. It is a good idea to draw each user path on a separate plan in a distinguishing colour. Arrowed lines should show the routes used in the area, taking account of any one-way systems, separate entrances and exits. A complete picture of the common and restricted routes will gradually emerge and help determine the sign wording and placement. It is also a good idea to look at the possible intersections of traffic, especially when signing emergency routes out of a building.

A well-placed identificational sign will often eliminate the need for directional signing. Directional signing is not usually needed when there is only one route available to the user, other than to confirm that the correct route has been chosen.

Informational and ornamental

These signs are location-specific; they are often viewed as landmarks by the user.

Statutory

Statutory signing is sometimes considered unexciting by designers, who feel they are restricted in their design options. This need not be the case. It is possible to produce elegant and considered signs in this category; the design of these signs, like all others, should be seen as a creative challenge.

Number of signs

People do not always act in a predictable manner, and the number and position of signs are often matters of intuition and experience, as well as logical planning! The aim is to provide the smallest feasible number of signs to meet the requirements of the directional system.

By now the designer should have a comprehensive plan of how the building is used, together with all the information required to use it efficiently. The position and wording of each individual sign is usually decided by the client, or client and designer together; the sign is then allocated a number. This information is listed and is known as the 'signing schedule'.

Production and manufacture

Once the signing schedule is complete, and the detailed design of each sign is finalized, the designer can proceed to organize production and manufacture of the signs themselves.

The manufacturer

Designer and client both need to be confident that the manufacturer can produce high-quality signs. In the

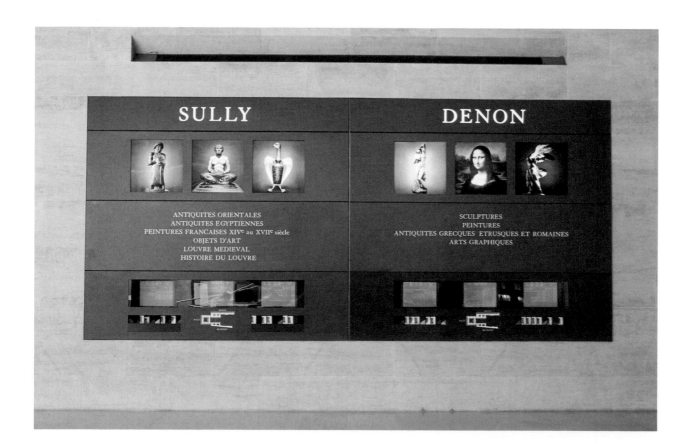

UK, the designer should determine whether the sign manufacturer is a member of the British Sign Association, and should look for the Quality Assurance registration of BS.5750, parts 1 and 2, ISO 9000 series (design, manufacturing and installation processes). Additionally, a good sign company will usually have a project manager to liaise with the designer or the main contractor. In the US, manufacturers may be industrial members of the SEGD.

The designer

In most situations the designer is the intermediary between client and manufacturer, a role which needs to be clearly explained to and understood by the client. The client places the order and agrees the terms and conditions with the sign manufacturer direct. As the details of the sign manufacture and fixings are not usually the designer's decision, he or she is generally exempt from any legal liability in this area. It is quite

◄ Sully and Denon are two of the neighbourhoods (*arrondissements*) that the designers Carbone Smolan Associates used as an orientation concept for the huge project of providing a visitor's information and sign system for the Grand Louvre in Paris.

► Designer Takenobu Igarashi considers the signing scheme for the Keio Hiyoshi Library, on the Keio University campus, Yokohama, Japan, to be one of his main achievements. The simple, elegant design of the signs is quite stunning and beautiful. There are references to paper-folding, and the effective juxtaposition of simple shapes is the very essence of Japanese design.

common, however, for the designer to assist or advise in the selection of manufacturers. The designer should check and approve full-size artwork and drawings, and where possible inspect signs at the manufacturer's premises before delivery and installation.

The prototype

If a very experimental sign has been designed, most manufacturers insist on producing a sign prototype, to scale, to see whether the sign will actually work. This is a wise precaution and investment for the designer, the manufacturer and the client. In some cases the manufacturer takes the risk along with the designer and the client. 399 Boylston Street, Boston, is one such example. The tempered-glass window had to be manufactured with the holes already in positionfor the acrylic lettering.

▲ Faultless sign installation is an essential part of the whole design process. This illustration provides an indication of the possible operation, and the necessary equipment.

◄ Here the Alliance and Leicester, London, are having an illuminated sign installed, to ensure corporate visibility.

► In a few short hours the sign is in working order. The letters sit happily on this curved building front, and the '+' symbol provides a colourful focus of attention for the whole sign.

It demanded perfect precision and, as Coco Raynes explains, 'Much depended on a manufacturer willing to go along and take the risk.'

Guarantees

Manufacturing guarantees usually include a performance specification for workmanship and the materials involved. A guarantee will normally last for between five and ten years.

Installation

The installation of signs is a significant part of the process. Signs can easily be damaged by transportation, handling and installation. The installation process should be professionally executed to safeguard the client's financial investment and the reputation of the designer. If new signs replace existing ones, the removal and disposal of the old signs

and 'making good' need to be completed before installing the new. If the sign system is very large, the need for temporary signing should be considered – usually PVC text on a temporary material. For larger jobs, good fixing crews are 'notoriously difficult to find', according to Hawes Signs Limited (UK). Most fixers are sub-contracted by the sign manufacturers, who have little or no control over the fixing teams; this is a potential disaster for the designer and client. Hawes Signs suggests the following points as part of a general checklist for assessing a potential sign manufacturer:

Checklist

- Experience and referrals
- Number of crews (directly employed/sub-contracted)
- Length of service of staff

- Number and location of qualified electricians/neon installers
- Location of crews
- Management structure especially number of supervisors
- Guarantees offered on workmanship
- Training
- Number and type of specialist vehicles
- Method of distribution
- Method of scheduling and setting of priorities

The designer should, where appropriate, supervise the installation of signs on site by arrangement with the sign manufacturer, advising the main contractor of visits.

One of the most impressive of all signs is the installation by Weber Design for the Al Fresco restaurant in downtown Denver. The sign itself is a metal ribbon which appears to curve effortlessly in and out of the windowless frames of the building facade. In fact, the original building had previously been gutted, leaving only the brick facade. The new glass and stucco front is set back from the brick, leaving the space in which to dangle the ribbon.

The main installation problem was how to attach the ribbon to the crumbling brickwork. After much deliberation the ribbon was installed by two metalworkers who formed the curve as they connected it to the building, using special fasteners. The ribbon was painted after it was installed. The 'Al Fresco' calligraphy is white hand-cut vinyl lettering. It took seven days of problem-solving on site, with the designers and the installers, to accomplish this very beautiful street sculpture. The sign has since become a lower-downtown 'landmark'.

The restaurant has been so successful that a second one has been opened. Working closely with the architects, Weber Design was able to integrate a three-dimensional aluminium ribbon, similar to the original, into the main entry facade. This primary sign is supplemented by two halo-illuminated logo signs, with exposed neon.

Maintenance

Maintenance is an area of signing that is often neglected. There are two key aspects: maintaining the hardware of the system, and sustaining the system's integrity.

▲ The Al Fresco ribbon is supplemented with additional logo signs. These are halo-illuminated, featuring exposed 'neon'.

◀ This gracious, sweeping sign by Weber Design, Denver, Colorado, is an example of an inspired design concept applied with sheer determination. Despite significant obstacles, installation was completed on time and to budget.

▼ Capitalizing on the success of the 'landmark' status of the first sign, a similar concept was applied to a freestanding 'pad' restaurant in a suburban retail centre, also in Denver.

The hardware

Maintaining the hardware protects the client's investment and visual identity. The best solution is to establish a preventative maintenance contract with a good manufacturer. Such a contract may cover the cleaning, replacement of components, and the emergency replacement of key signs if accidentally damaged or vandalized. It is essential to maintain electrical signs for safety and appearance. Electrical signs are dramatically affected by partial illumination, missing components or dirt. If the signs are to be maintained by the client, the designer or manufacturer should detail exactly how and when this is to be done.

The design manual

A design manual is usually a 'book', designed for the client, which may have a number of functions. It can be used to describe the implementation of a new signing system to employees; as a design guide by client staff in the application of a visual identity; for maintenance staff to reorder signs in the corporate style; or even as a persuasive or political tool. A sign design manual is particularly useful for clients whose premises have continually changing internal and often external environments, which therefore need changes in their sign systems. These changes can be managed, and the integrity of the system maintained, by the client's, implementation of the signing recommendations contained in the manual, though naturally, if entirely new types of signs are required a designer will be needed.

Design manuals have become a hot issue in recent years, and cynical observers suggest that they are unneccesary and may even be used as vehicles for graphic designers to make money on the back of a signing project. The need for and specific role of a manual should be properly determined; a good design consultancy will advise the client accordingly. A design manual may be a statement of company policy, attitude or intention; it may also indicate a commitment to design and in some cases safety.

Feedback and project evaluation

If a system fails badly, there is likely to be immediate feedback from the client. But even if a system succeeds in the manner predicted it is useful to evaluate it after a period of use. A good guide is to see whether the users add to the signs or change them. The designer should also look at the physical condition of the signs to see whether they have been subjected to vandalism or excessive or unexpected weathering. It may be that people have not responded to the signs in the expected manner, that there have been changes in the way the project operates, or even that some signs have been badly designed, manufactured or installed. The designer may want to recommend changes or additions. He or she will also learn from any unexpected uses or abuses of the system, adding to the growing body of knowledge of signs and sign systems and allowing future designs to improve continually. It shows a caring attitude towards the client and the work – part of the growing trend towards cooperative working relationships.

Case study:

▲ The illuminated 'IBM' at the top of the tower building is a direct statement about the company.

In 1983, Pentagram was approached by IBM's architectural team to undertake a complete signing system for Tour Pascal, the new European headquarters, named after Blaize Pascal, inventor of a mechanical calculating machine using the principles which eventually lead to the computers of the twentieth century.

Tour Pascal epitomises IBM: situated in La Defence, the high technology district of Paris, the granite-faced, interlinked twin towers are unassuming and uncompromisingly modern. Pentagram analysed the problems and the requirements for the signing of the 52 floors and 1800 offices, as well as all the other facilities, such as conference rooms, restaurants, car parking, executive suites and communal areas. For this project the signs were reconciled into four main categories: identificational, directional, informational and statutory.

Having looked at the existing, standard, changeable sign systems available, one was found which was suitable for adaption for the individual office signs, which formed a major part of the programme. The system had to be flexible due to the high staff turnover of 40 per cent annually (IBM Europe's HQ is mainly staffed by personnel seconded from their national companies). A system was developed allowing names to be changed on individual offices and facilities, by replacing plates in a permanent surround.

▼ **The identification letters for the floors were cut in the very clear and legible Times New Roman out of polished stainless steel.**

The interior sign were required to act as part of the interior design. The intention was to compliment the quality and colour of the environment. Colour coding was introduced to distinguish between the two towers of Tour Pascal, either red or blue on a beige background - the IBM house colour. Times New Roman was chosen for the typeface. The signs for public areas were made of polished stainless steel, and a number of special signs were designed additional to the sign system.

A key part of the sign programme was the manufacture and installation of the 5000 signs for the premises. Soon after the sign programme was initiated, Alan Fletcher (a Pentagram partner) was asked to design a series of posters to decorate the walls of the offices, as an interim measure before the art-buying schedule for the building had been completed. Pentagram also undertook several ancillary projects, including the design of an exhibition and a series of leaflets describing the new facilities and their location.

IBM's Tour Pascal

◄ **A flexible system for name-plates caters for the high turnover of staff at the IBM headquarters.**

▶ A close-up of this 'Enter' sign for a parking garage in the Solana Business Park shows the careful three-dimensional use of both the lettering and its metal background support (see page 94).

3 Symbols and wayfinding

3

Symbols and wayfinding

► The combination of colour and material make these parking signs very strong features within the overall architectural composition; the message is clear and unmistakable.

Sign design inevitably involves the use of symbols. These key elements of communication may not necessarily be originated by the designer, but it is the designer who must use them to maximum effect, capitalizing on their power to communicate. The concept of 'wayfinding', also covered in this chapter, takes the communication factor a step further, exploring the whole field of sign interpretation in the context of directional messages.

Symbols

Symbols in general demand the expertise of graphic designers who specialize in corporate identity, but the translation of a given symbol into three dimensions for use as a sign then becomes the job of the environmental graphic designer. The term 'symbol' used here includes pictograms, although the words 'pictogram' and 'symbol' originally had quite different meanings. A pictogram is a representation of an object: for example, a picture of a person which identifies the particular users of a toilet facility. Abstract or arbitrary symbols such as letters, numerals and signs have no visual relationship with the objects or concepts they represent, but communicate an idea. Although most people in a given culture understand many symbols, their meanings must be learned.

Use of symbols in signing

Symbols in the broader context are usually used as aids to directional signing, or as identificational signs. They are very commonly used, particularly in transportational facilities, zoos, and for special one-off events such as the Olympic Games,

which require information to be conveyed to many different nationalities. At one time an international language of symbols was suggested in the hope of solving fundamental problems of communication. However, symbols have proved not to be the panacea that designers once thought they might be. There are many inherent problems with their design.

International symbols

There are no 'international' symbols or standards, although a number of conventions are understood internationally. The whole area is one of duplication and confusion; there are many symbol systems, and no one system has been, or is likely to be, adopted for use in all countries for specific situations, such as international airports. Internationally, many graphic designers have adopted the 1974 US Department of Transportation symbols coordinated by the American Institute of Graphic Arts (AIGA) but that is the limit of the standardization. In the US, these symbols have not even been successfully implemented on federal highways.

The design and implementation of an international language of symbols appears an insurmountable problem. Whether it is necessary is

► Part of the sign system for the Solana Business Park, this galloping blue and yellow stallion, with his splendid bronze mane and tail, points to a sign showing the way to Highway 114. In the body of the horse several squares are punched out on three sides and peeled back on the fourth side.

an interesting question. The obvious need is for research into symbols for situations where speed of recognition is essential; where, for example there are issues of public safety.

Design problems

The problems of symbol design are many and complicated. The design of systems of signs using symbols is a relatively recent idea, and many people find difficulty with the concept itself. Designers almost always make design decisions based on their own experience. Often, incorrect assumptions are made about the knowledge of the users, and therefore their ability to understand the symbols. Assumed universality is another problem; the designer cannot assume that a symbol which is widely understood in one culture will be in another. Margaret Mead, an anthropologist, reminds designers that the skull and crossbones does not mean poison, nor does red connote danger, to all populations of the world.

It is sometimes thought that symbols are more effective when accompanied by words. Not only does this rather defeat the purpose, it also neglects multilingual considerations, which can cause immense design problems. The designer needs to consider which languages to use, and how to communicate the idea efficiently, incorporating the languages and the symbols. The current wisdom is that the effectiveness of symbols is strictly limited, that they are more easily understood when representing an object than an idea, and that they are useless unless part of a coherent system.

Effective use of symbols

There are situations, including those in which public safety is of prime concern, such as roads, where symbols can be used as signs or as parts of signs to great effect. Museums, country parks, walkway systems, zoos, exhibitions and so on, are absolutely suitable for the use of creative symbols. Symbols may be fun, add interest, be educational or simply be used as elements of colour in

an environment. They may be used to standardize and unify a location or a series of locations, or express and amplify differences.

The most visually pleasing symbol systems tend to be those concerned with a single classification of recognizable images, such as sporting events and animals. When dealing with several symbols the designer must maintain clear communication and at the same time establish visual consistency. The development of even one symbol is a challenging task for the experienced graphic designer. The design of a system of consistent symbols to be used as signs is an extraordinarily complex task, and should only be undertaken by an experienced professional environmental graphic designer.

Evaluation of symbols

Designers need to evaluate their symbols to see whether people will understand them. This is very hard to do without systematic testing. For many designers, thorough testing and evaluation is not usually a practical option. To be sure of a design requires investment of considerable time and expense. But, as a minimum, designers should consult each other, the client and the identified users. The following series of evaluative questions may be asked of the proposed symbol design:

Semantic
This refers to the relationship between the visual image and its meaning. Does the symbol need to represent the message clearly to people of many cultures? How might it be misunderstood by the users?

Syntactic
This refers to the relationship of one visual image to another. How well does the symbol fit into the entire system of other symbols?

Pragmatic
This refers to the relationship between the symbol and its users. Can it be seen clearly under varying conditions and when reproduced in various sizes?

N★RTH

Wayfinding

Wayfinding is literally the ability to find one's way to a given destination; to navigate and orientate oneself. Romedi Passini, author of Wayfinding in Architecture, describes wayfinding as 'the strategies that people use to find their way in familiar or new settings, based on their perceptual and cognitive abilities and habits.' It also involves the way in which people receive and assimilate environmental information. In design terms, wayfinding is largely an academic discipline, but it does have great potential for the practical design of particular signs and sign systems.

Wayfinding theory

Wayfinding theory is based on the certain fact that people have difficulty finding their way to given destinations, and not because of ignorance or stupidity. The problem causes emotional distress, and wastes time. It has been estimated that in an average 800-bed hospital, some 8000 hours per annum are spent by the staff redirecting visitors.

Passini's strategies are represented by three interdependent processes:

■ Decision making, which leads to a plan of action – how I am going to get to my destination;

■ Decision execution, which converts the plan into action or behaviour;

■ Information processing (involving environmental perceptions and cognition) which allows the other two processes to occur.

Environmental information

Environmental information may be divided into three categories:

■ Architectural information is contained or inherent in the built environment, whether the user is in a building or outside. A building shape or layout may be difficult or easy to read. But even difficult buildings have a wealth of information present in the details: stairs, lifts, corridors doorways, floor coverings and so on are all landmarks used to determine the way to a given destination.

■ Graphic information, which may be further subdivided into general information about building tenants, directions to destinations in a building, and the identification of those destinations.

■ Verbal information includes the sorts of information that can be imparted by passers-by, security guards, occupants, and self-help telephones. David Canter, a pioneer researcher in

this field, suggests that there is insufficient knowledge of the different and preferred ways in which people assess information. However, many users seem to prefer to talk to someone rather than look at a sign. Conversation is interactive; a route can be described in terms of landmarks familiar to a user who can ask further questions for clarification. Additionally, a person can indicate how confident he or she is about the information and indicate how up to date it is.

Signs fall into the first and second categories and are fundamental to an individual's wayfinding strategy. If wayfinding has been implicitly recognized as a design priority, the sign designer must work out how best to answer to the challenge. There are many diverse, appropriate responses.

Wayfinding designers

On a practical level environmental graphic designers and architects need to work together as wayfinding designers. Architecture should not be considered one element and the signing quite another, the roles should be complementary. Integration on this level is rare; designers need to overcome their reluctance to work with architects and, crucially, architects need to withdraw their indifference to environmental graphic designers. Contrary to the

◄ ▲ ▼ These orientational signs for the Pedway, in Edmonton, designed by Lance Wyman combine letterforms and symbols within each word. The symbols refer to Edmonton's past history, giving a simple easily understood message.

belief of many architects, the addition of signs to an environment is not consistent with a lack of architectural integrity or design failure.

Focus on the user

Designers need to be aware of the different categories of users (detailed in Chapter 2), and adopt a more sophisticated approach towards their requirements. All users need the right information, appropriately communicated, at the right time and place. Some designers unconsciously design environments comprehensible only to themselves. Focusing on the user will encourage designers not to make this error.

Research

Designers should be aware of the wayfinding research that is currently taking place. In the US they can help themselves by becoming members of the SEGD, and sharing their own empirical design findings with others. Researchers can assist designers by making a conscious effort to have the results and conclusions of their studies published as widely as possible. The whole profession needs to be more open and encourage its maturation by the free-flow of information and exchange of ideas.

Gerald Weisman is a wayfinding researcher. Part of his research entails an evaluation of the proportion of people who become confused when faced with a new environment, such as a hospital, airport or shopping centre. Weisman describes how environmental simulation can be a valuable tool in this process. It allows the researcher to test different wayfinding theories and systematically evaluate people's responses to them. Wayfinding solutions can be methodically tested, helping the designer form information-based decisions and practical solutions to wayfinding problems.

The debate

The field of wayfinding is new and developing; there are issues to discuss and problems to be resolved: combining aesthetic interests with legible wayfinding information; measuring wayfinding responses; assessing the commercial benefits of legible environments for developers and so on. Designers need to become involved in, and where possible contribute to, current debates. Wayfinding offers many exciting possibilities for signs in the future and will undoubtedly aid designers in their decision-making.

The future

Fundamental to the large-scale growth of wayfinding is its inclusion in the educational curricula of architects and environmental graphic designers. Wayfinding is taught in some architectural schools in the US, one in Canada and, as far as is known, none in the UK. The general crisis in environmental graphic design education is only beginning to be addressed by the research of the SEGD: wayfinding is not yet on the agenda.

The future of wayfinding is not assured. Designers need to be increasingly willing to spend some of their time as missionaries for better wayfinding practices. They need to educate not only themselves, but also those who are responsible for educational programmes and those who directly shape the environment. Such people include educators, city planners, developers, architects, designers and builders.

Paul Arthur, an authority on wayfinding, sees future trends shifting away from specific problem-solving in relation to projects, towards the design and development of more general wayfinding systems: 'By developing workable systems that remove the drudgery from the development of a wayfinding system by non-professionals, designers will be making a real contribution to the quality of life in our society.'

In high stress, and in confusing architectural environments, such wayfinding systems would be a timely, revolutionary contribution. However, in the majority of the projects, uniqueness of place should be respected. Effective, sophisticated responses to environmental stimuli will create more interesting and enriching environments for all user groups.

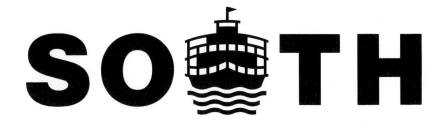

Lance Wyman, principal of Lance Wyman Ltd, based in Manhattan, is a specialist in the design of symbols for environmental graphic design projects. His most noted work includes signing for the 1968 Olympic Games in Mexico City, informational signing for Mexico City's subway, graphic and signing for the National Zoo in Washington DC, and a visual information system for the Mall in Washington DC.

His recent projects are distinguished by the educational use of symbols within sign systems, designed for pedestrian walkways. In recent years, major North American cities have begun to add climate-controlled connecting bridges and tunnels between buildings, to form pedestrian walkway systems. These systems are enclosed, city-wide mazes that offer few views of city landmarks for orientation. 'The Skyway' in Minneapolis and St Paul, 'The Skywalk' in Des Moines, Cincinnati and Milwaukee, 'The Pedestrian System' in Dallas, 'The Connection' in Houston, 'The Pedway' in Edmonton and 'The Plus 15' in Calgary are all examples.

These walkway systems are extensive enough to warrant their own transportation graphics. The function of the graphic system is similar to that of other transportation systems. A walkway usually has a name and a logo. It has signs to identify entrances from the street, a route map to give an overview of where it goes, and directional signing to help users find their way. Orientation is a problem in pedestrian systems; a sense of direction is needed every step of the way to avoid getting hopelessly lost.

Lance Wyman Ltd has designed the graphic systems for The Pedway and The Plus 15 and is also part of a consultant team on the Toronto Underground.

Lance Wyman used the graphic device of dividing the signs into three, clearly distinguishing which of three levels the pedestrian is on, in this effective system designed for the Pedway in Edmonton.

The Pedway
The Pedway, Edmonton, operates on three levels: above street, street level and below street. Maps showing Pedway entrances and levels, street names and landmarks, are displayed with compass points for orientation. The signs situated on the outside of entrances indicate which level the Pedway will be on.

North is depicted by a symbol of the North Star. Edmonton is traditionally known as the 'Gateway to the North'. For bush pilots, prospectors and explorers, Edmonton was the last place at which one could to stock up with supplies before continuing the journey North. South is depicted by the symbol of a paddle-wheeled steamboat, named The City of Edmonton, which used to run up and down the Saskatchewan River, just south of Edmonton's downtown. East is depicted by a symbol of the oil refineries which lie to the east of Edmonton. The oil industry established Edmonton as the 'Oil Capital of Canada'. West is depicted by the spectacular Canadian Rockies which rise to the west of the city.

The integration of these 'landmark' pictograms with the letters is a masterly device designed to orientate and educate. Even visitors quickly become familiar with Edmonton. The graphics are familiar, friendly and easily

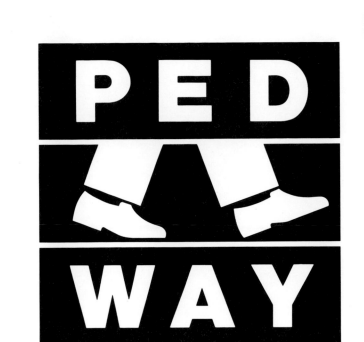

understood. The system is simple and effective, and this effectiveness will undoubtedly have a positive impact on the appropriate use of symbols within the design of other transportation systems.

Lance Wyman offers the following suggestions in designing a pedestrian graphics system

■ A clear diagramatic map. This should be displayed frequently throughout the walkway and always orientated correctly. If the map borders are strongly marked with North, South, East and West, and the name of the next building in each direction is clearly shown, the map can function as both large compass and directional sign.

■ Bridges and tunnel entrances should be clearly signed with the compass direction and the next immediate destination.

■ Orientation should be clearly indicated along routes from one bridge or tunnel to another especially at turns. The sign device used should appear frequently.

Another consideration is the relationship of signs to their environment. Walkways link and pass through a variety of different environments. They not only have to show the

The Pedway

way but be compatible with downtown offices, retail centres, museums, theatres, restaurants, hotels, parking facilities and so on. The designer has to consider the integrity of the system and the individual signs within the system in terms of size, material, surface texture, degree of detailing and so on. Naturally, many pedestrian graphics signs will be viewed from very short distances.

When designing walkway signs, the symbology, typography, colour and sign layouts should be consistent, so that the public can become familiar with the system and its messages. This will also enable sign messages to be integrated into existing sign and map structures where appropriate. The consistency of the system should always be considered when using existing structures.

When designing sign structures, it is best to allow for a range of colours and natural materials. A compatible colour, a naturally finished bronze or stainless-steel surface might be more appropriate than astandard system colour within existing architectural environments.

Case study:

◀ **The splendid red and lavender wolf shown here howls into the Texas sky. Like the horse, the body of the wolf also has a punched-out design, adding to the three-dimensional effect.**

Solana is a fascinating wayfinding project. Environmental graphic designers and architects worked together in an extraordinarily creative collaboration to produce what may well come to be regarded as a masterpiece of design.

Solana is a business park complex. It is the result of a masterplan for joint developers Maguire Thomas Partners and IBM Corp., by four designers: Ricardo Legorreta of Mexico City and Romaldo Giurgola of New York for the architecture and planning, Peter Walker of San Francisco for the landscape and land planning, and Debra Nichols of Skidmore, Owings and Merrill, San Francisco, for the environmental design and graphics.

Solana, meaning 'sunny place' in Spanish, is a mixed-use 900-acre development in Texas. It straddles a highway which runs between Dallas and Fort Worth. The first phase, already built, represents 3 million square feet. Ultimately, the complex will cover around 7 million square feet. The predominant building types will be offices and research and development areas. There is a Village Centre which includes a retail complex, a sports complex and a 200-room hotel. The raw site was a beautiful Texas setting of open rural landscape, edged in rolling hills and oak groves.

The programme for the signing had to meet two basic requirements: to identify major intersections and tenant areas, and to provide directional information. Overriding these was the developer's intention to create a cohesive 'community', rather than simply a collection of roads, buildings and land-scaping. In the words of Tom Allen, senior vice-president at Maguire Thomas, their desire was to have a 'mixed-use and office environment with no thought of maximizing the use of land, but allowing the land to shine through'.

The project is special for many reasons. One of the most impressive aspects is the degree to which the usual distinctions between different types of designer have been broken down. Legorreta worked with forms and colours which find counterparts in art and graphic design. Legorreta and Walker designed a punctuated wall around the freeway interchange, providing access to Solana. This sculptural element marks the entry and creates what the architects describe as the 'foyer'. The buildings also include large sculptural elements, such as 'pylons', to reinforce their identity and help people recognize the site from the freeway.

Ideas like these encouraged a creative and 'fresh' approach to the signing. The design team, headed by Debra Nichols, began by visiting examples of signing with similar materials and environmental conditions. Simultaneously, the graphics masterplan was developed. The team identified the directional needs, traffic intersections and so on, and prepared a sign-type inventory. The idea was that the directional signs should act as landmarks, and maintain their interest and attractiveness even when seen every day.

Having decided on an art-based approach to the problem, the team began to look at images of native southwest art. Nichols was particularly impressed by the recurring animal imagery of the Huichol Indians: 'The purity was so

Solana

▶ **The extraordinary birds, here and overleaf, which sit on brightly coloured posts, are reminiscent of crafted metal weathervanes still found in America's heartland. Both point to the Sports Club, from different directions.**

attractive – the thought of signs as sculpture in the form of a completely new image vocabulary at the site seemed to be compelling.' The team started to discuss three-dimensional symbols to mark place and distance. These detailed, figurative signs, which would be frequently seen, would act as orientation tools, and would be visual forerunners and thereafter constant reminders of the richness and details of the architecture.

Nichols also commented on the historical precedence of animal forms for signs and sign markers, such as the weather vanes and shop signs of rural America. The Huichol animal forms underwent several layers of refinement; Nichols wanted to reflect a modernist spirit. Details such as perforations and regular geometric patterning made direct reference to the work of the other designers.

▲ **Level two of the Village Centre is identified by a number and a colourful decorative geometric panel. The designers took their cue from the architecture - refined and graceful in its simplicity.**

There are six animals at Solana: three freestanding twelve-foot-high mammals (a steer, a horse and a wolf) at major intersections, and three five-foot high birds (a road-runner, a bluejay and an owl) on posts at secondary intersections. The selection of animals is indige-nous to the region. Their colours are inspired by the rich hues of the southwest, as well as Legorreta's Mexican palette. Oxidized metal details were used to give a slightly weathered look. Full-size mock-ups were tested and approved by a very enthusiastic client.

The rest of the directional signing 'fell into place' and became extremely simple. Directional, street and regulatory signs were designed to avoid competing with other elements in the environment, particularly the landscaping. Directional signs are post-and-panel constructions and street-signs mere posts. The traffic regulatory signs simply follow the state standard.

Legorreta's design for the retailing complex in the Village Centre uses planar elements such as long, triangular walls to set the character and define the space. Its simplicity made the signs more important – almost a foreground ele-ment in the composition. 'The signs are bigger than usual, with unusual shape and strong colours. We place them in odd places, in terms of conventional [signing], but in places which work well for the building...The sign becomes the focal point of the design, which is something the retailers desire.'

▲ Here the signs and the architecture are seen in context – the red stone entry foyer at the highway interchange together with a panel and post sign. It would be difficult to imagine a more complementary design - the effect is quite stunning.

Nichols and Legorreta worked closely together on the car-park signing for Solana. The genesis of the collaboration was the decision to place crenellat-ed metal entry and exit signs as cut-outs for those functions of the buildings. Like the retail signing, these elements are sculptural as well as functional. When Legorreta saw the design he strengthened it by adding colour at the openings. The resulting combination makes these very strong elements in the composition, as well as clearly defining the entrance and exit.

The identification of the car-park cores was the second design problem. Working with different colours and patterns, Nichols added a series of metal grilles to decorate the openings that Giurgola had placed in each of the stair towers. In the Village car-park, tile designs based on sand drawings decorate each of the elevator lobbies, and visually identify which building is being served. In another car-park for IBM, the cores are marked by large metal sculptures.

The interior building signing uses the same oxidized metal and copper leaf that is used to characterize the animal signs. The building signs are recti-linear cut-metal cans with cut-out letters.

This project is an outstanding testimony to design excellence. The collabora-tion of the designers was extraordinary and rewarding. The quality of the signing work is quite magnificent. All the design elements work together as a unified whole.

Case study:

▲ **The warm red and grey tones of this orientational plan for the Ancient Egyptian gallery blend in with the natural materials of marble and wood used in the palace.**

In 1985 the Louvre, Paris launched a competition to design a new signing system for the museum, incorporating I.M. Pei's controversial glass pyramid. The large structure of the Louvre palace is made up of several different buildings constructed by the rulers of France over the centuries. It now houses 60,000 works of art. Navigation in and between the buildings was very problematic. As a gift to the people of France, President Mitterand decided to renovate the Louvre in line with its function as an art gallery and museum. The official name of the project was Le Grand Louvre.

After an immense amount of work, the New York-based design firm, Carbone Smolan Associates won the competition with their proposal. The problem was to design a workable sign system which interfaced with the new Cour Napoleon, the central court bounded on three sides by the Louvre's buildings, and its centrally located glass pyramid, taking into account the modernity of the new structure and the classicism of the palace. Most importantly the signs had to be efficient in getting the people where they wanted to be.

The problem as Carbone and Chief Project Designer John Plunkett saw it, was to 'design a clean and understandable program of informational and directional signs for what was essentially a moving target.' The designers viewed the job as almost impossible, due to the renovation and relocation of exhibits in the Louvre.

Grand Louvre

▲ **This is the main exterior orientation plan to the pyramid. The designers simplified the existing maps of the Louvre, which tended to be too complex to follow. This timely improvement anticipated the increased museum attendance.**

The solution was generated, initially, by looking at the problem in a totally new way, by asking how people find their way around complex problems, like driving on the highway for the first time. Computers, abstract maps and paths were considered, and rejected. People had to first accept a system they could understand, so they would later embrace it.

The concept

The solution was to look at the Louvre as a city with each floor of a wing in the museum as *arrondissements* (neighbourhoods) and galleries as addresses. Each wing of the museum was divided into equal neighbourhoods, and levels were colour-coded. The signs were supplemented by a multi-lingual, hand-held paper guide, indicating the division of *arrondissements* and specific locations and attractions. The great advantage of this wayfinding system was seen to be its strong personality. Collections could be moved without the need to modify the permanent sign system, just as in a city, the buildings on a street may be altered while the street numbers remain the same.

The signs

A classical visual approach was rejected in favour of a simpler solution, reflecting the new foundations of the museum. The client indicated that , 'the new Rennaissance [has to] function for the next 100 years.' The signs were designed as a contrast to the environment. All were variations on the square. Sandblasted steel and aluminium combined with glass were chosen as the main sign materials. I.M. Pei has chosen a similar sandblasted steel for the pyramid interior.

A simple, yet revolutionary, approach to this complex signing problem makes the signing for the Louvre a big wayfinding success. It has made one of the largest, most complex structures in Europe welcoming and understandable. It is a significant contribution to the accessibility of an important part of France's cultural heritage.

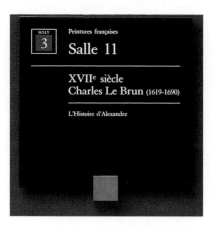

◄ A wall-mounted orientation plan.

► A wall-mounted identificational sign in the French painting department.

◄ Each of the three main wings of the Louvre were assigned names, Sully, Denon and Richlieu. This is the major identificational sign at the entrance to Pavillion Sully. It is made from glass, with metal letters attached.

▼ Carbone Smolan's sign system is immediately discernible on entering the foyer, standing out clearly against the neutral tones of the marble.

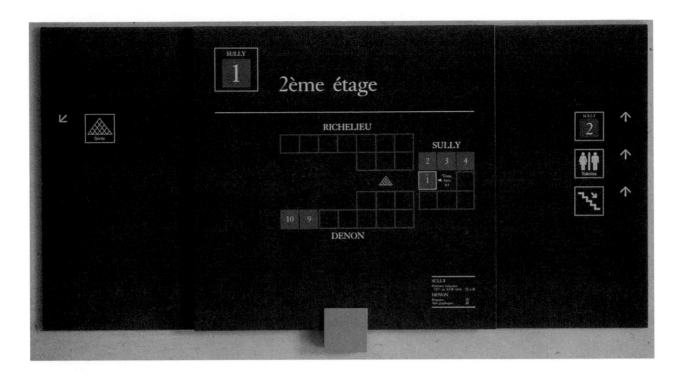

One of the most common and familiar wayfinding problems is the multi-storey parking garage. Usually an anonymous monolithic building with no distinguishing features, once inside the individual and the car quickly lose their identity and bringing the two successfully together again is a challenge to the designer. Effective sign systems are not only essential to the function of the space but can also be used to add character to the building.

One of the most original and imaginative solutions to the 'garage problem' is perhaps the system designed by Gottschalk and Asch International for the Contraves Manufacturing Company in Zurich, Switzerland, completed in 1980 as part of the building expansion programme. The garage holds 600 cars and is used by employees of the research electronics firm.

The designers began with an alphabetical labelling of parking floors and developed this as an identification system by using the letters as the initials of well-known historical personalities, literally adding 'character' to each level. Most of the people chosen are scientists or philosophers, some with electronics connections - Greta Garbo is the notable exception. On every level, a steel-framed poster panel displays the initial large letter and a brief biographical note against a silk-screened portrait of the figure. The graphic style, using Univers as the typeface, is consistent throughout, but different colours add variety and warmth, and further differentiate the space.

The prize-winning design has also been a great success with the users, who are reported to feel that their employer 'is making an effort to help them'. The designers, in turn, credit their clients for 'having the guts to let us do it'.

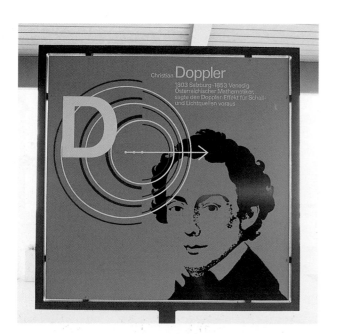

◄ Every parking level is identified by a letter and personality which help to give character to an otherwise impersonal building.

▲ ◄ Clear directional signs are particularly important during the construction phase.

Contraves Parking Garage

► The excitement of a city at night, here Tokyo's shopping centre of Shibuya-ku, is created by the colour and movement of illuminated signs.

4 Illuminated and electronic signing

4

Illuminated and electronic signing

▶ The musical *Cats* is a spectacular success. This is the main sign for the London production. Using neon most effectively, it looks stunning in its West End night-time environment, and due to its size and careful positioning it can be seen from considerable distances.

Illuminated and electronic signs are an exciting addition to any environment; the light they emit gives them a distinct vitality – a life of their own. A designer who is familiar with the language and use of illuminated and electronic signing will find that experimentation and investigation are key factors in this relatively new field, where techniques and equipment are almost daily becoming more sophisticated.

Illuminated signs

Lighting for signs is often ignored. Even when it has clearly been considered, the results are often adequate at best. Excellent lighting for signs is uncommon. One of the main reasons is the lack of education in the subject; college courses in general lighting are a relatively new phenomenon, and this specialized aspect is not taught to designers from any discipline. Nevertheless, designers should be as well-versed as possible in the general techniques of illuminated signing, the basic principles of artificial light and the different types of light. Colour rendering, reflections, shadows, the amount of light, power needs and maintenance all need to be taken into consideration.

But even professionals get few opportunities to learn about this subject. Technical information is not readily accessible or digestible except from 'manufacturers' catalogues, and there are few occasions when a designer may experiment with the vast selection of fittings and lamps available. Staff in lighting shops often know little about the merchandise, and the usual display methods make it impossible to view one light source or fitting at a time, making accurate observation difficult.

Undoubtedly one of the best ways to learn about lighting is through 'hands-on' experience and careful observation. Designers are using lights and signs in an ever more experimental way, but are only just beginning to understand their creative potential. As Nicolete Gray so rightly said in 1960, 'The real opportunity for flamboyant expression is the illuminated letter but so far it has been done with little skill or daring.' However, manufacturers and designers are now collaborating on projects, continually pushing back the boundaries of achievement and knowledge, and the future promises further advances in fibre optics, energy efficiency and conservation.

▼ The Fuji Building, Times Square, New York, is a dynamic company statement, exactly appropriate in this exciting environment. This enormous, expensive sign, requiring constant maintenance, is a visual commitment to being brighter, bigger and better than the competition.

Design possibilities

The possibilities available through the use of light are enormous. Illuminated signs have a high degree of visual impact. The strength of the message is reinforced by the illumination. En masse, in places like Piccadilly Circus and Times Square, the signs become the environment. The illumination creates a dynamic, vibrant atmosphere. Buildings are even referred to by the name of their sign – the Coca Cola building, the Fuji building and so on. Naturally, lighting tends to be most effective at night and when employed in interiors, as the designer can manipulate a greater range of tone and contrast. A sign which is continuously lit, however, makes a continual statement.

On a smaller scale the visual impact of illumination is exploited by restauranteurs, retailers and the entertainment industry. In the US there are a great many illuminated exterior signs. 'Dunkin Donuts', for instance, an American fast-food outlet with a distinctive orange and pink neon sign, is one of the most obvious navigational landmarks in any neighbourhood. When signs become part of a city environment and are seen as characteristic of 'commercial archaeology', they often become 'designated' as such, and maintained by city or state authorities. In interior situations, multiple illuminated signs are also common where appropriate. In Europe too, the trend towards increased illuminated signing is clear.

At its simplest the direction of artificial light can help guide the eye towards a sign, or make a sign stand out against its background. Where there is a visibility problem, illuminated signs can help with speedy identification.

Light is commonly used to create or enhance a mood. An external restaurant sign subtly lit with warm tungsten light will look welcoming and invite patronage. Light can be directed and focused quite specifically to achieve the designer's intended look, with well-chosen

◀ This beautiful carved, gilded, wooden sign for a restaurant in Great Queen Street, London, is hidden under a canopy and lit by warm spotlights. The subtlety of this restaurant's lettering is suggestive of its fine, delicate Indian cuisine.

▼ This lovely little theatre in Cambridge, England, illuminates its bold lettering with soft tungsten light. Although large, this sign is appropriate for its function and environment, aptly dramatizing the nature of the building without being over-pretentious.

lamps and fittings. Particular material qualities may be enhanced by the sympathetic use of light. The quality and detail of the gilded, wooden letters in the exquisite fascia sign for Bhatti, a restaurant in London, are good examples.

Where a sign has a strong sculptural or three-dimensional form, light plays a vital role in the viewer's understanding and perception. Light can dramatically alter tone and mood. The individual letters of Opera, a popular theatrical restaurant, are lit by coloured light. The sign is exactly appropriate whilst being witty and fun. Buildings too are often illuminated, many as physical symbols of corporate identity.

Signs can be fun. Fiorucci, for example, employs some of the most creative and diverse retailing illuminated signing. Stores throughout the world illuminate the word 'Fiorucci' in individual and exciting ways.

Such an approach expresses the individuality of each store and the clothes within, whilst reassuring the customer of Fiorucci quality and service.

Advance consideration

Illuminated signs are expensive in relation to other signs and must be planned and budgeted for well in advance. The ideal situation is to be working with architects and interior designers at the outset of a scheme. Usually, however, a designer will be asked to design a sign for a particular position in, on, or near an existing building.

Characteristics of light

Within the electro-magnetic spectrum, the eye is stimulated by a tiny range known as visible light. All light has identifiable characteristics.

▼ Fiorucci, as always, demonstrate their flair for dynamic retail signing. This London store uses multicoloured cold-cathode light in a stunning display. It is attractive, fashionable and fun.

◄ The fascia panel for this New York
▼ Fiorucci store spells the name by the
use of large serif cut-out letterforms with
a kinetic input, starting empty and
quickly filling with multi-coloured cold
cathode bars. The movement is
eyecatching and entertaining.

▲ The coloured lighting makes this lettering for one of London's fashionable, theatrical restaurants quite extraordinary. The yellow and green make a distinctive combination, which is underlined by the embellishment of traditional tungsten lightbulbs.

These are: colour, physical distribution, direction and intensity. Light will be somewhere between perfectly focused (hard-edged) and non-focused (soft-edged). Visible light itself is composed of many colours (or wavelengths of light), together perceived to be white light.

Types of light

The sun is the source of all natural light, but light can also be made artificially. Natural and artificial light can be used as ambient or feature lighting. Artificial light can be produced electrically and electronically. Electronic systems, which include light-emitting diodes, liquid-crystal displays, light-reflecting displays, split-flap messages and television systems, are discussed later in this chapter. Electrical methods include fluorescent, incandescent, high-intensity discharge and cold-cathode lamps (although these are usually fluorescent).

Fluorescent light

Fluorescent lamps are lamps utilizing the passage of electricity through a gas or vapour, to produce light

directly, or by means of a fluorescent phosphor. The first fluorescent lamp to be commercially available was introduced to the public at the New York World Fair in 1939, although fluorescent lamps with cold cathodes had been produced since the mid-30s.

A standard fluorescent lamp has cathodes at either end, which are initially heated by passing an electric current through them. This raises the temperature to red heat, at which point a special emissive coating (usually barium oxide) releases a large number of electrons. These are accelerated along the tube by an electric field, and collide with atoms of mercury vapour that are present in the tube. The energy imparted by these collisions increases the energy in the electrons associated with the mercury atoms, raising their energy levels. As the electrons move back to their original levels, they give up this energy in the form of visible light, as well as ultraviolet radiation (which the eye cannot see). The phosphor coating inside the lamp absorbs the ultraviolet radiation and gives off more visible light. This is called fluorescing. The colour of the light is dependent on the make-up of the phosphor coating.

Fluorescent lighting is often used for general illumination. Fluorescent tubes are 'linear sources': the light is transmitted evenly along the length and around the circumference of the tube. Therefore the transmitted light is quite uniform. These lamps are used for internally-lit signs, such as box signs and fascias.

Internally illuminated signs

Signs which have an internal light source are commonly called internally illuminated signs. They usually consist of a plastic box within a metal frame, which acts as a support and container for the concealed electrical installation. The sign face and a light source are installed inside the frame. Ideally, these illuminated signs are sealed against weather and insects attracted by the light. This requires the use of a close-mesh screen over any openings in the light 'box'. Even so, supposedly sealed units have been found full of small insects. Attention should be paid to all components, wire, switching, ballasts and fixtures to ensure that each is designed to handle the desired lighting wattage. Lighting units that develop high temperatures must be adequately ventilated and spaced from materials with a tendency to be damaged by heat.

Even illumination and brightness of signs

A rough guide, given materials with average diffusion properties, is that, in order to achieve even illumination, fluorescent tubes should be placed not more than one foot (30.5 cm) apart, and at least four inches (10 cm) away from the back of the

▼ The fascia sign for Top Shop, Top Man, in Cambridge, England, makes a particular feature of its fine sculptural, identificational name. It is whacky and fun, whilst remaining legible. The shadows add to the dramatic effect.

face of the sign. Generally, painted surfaces provide better diffusion than self-coloured plastics; the lamps may be placed closer to the front face without having to reduce their spacing. If a deep box is made, the lamps may be spaced further apart to achieve the same evenness of illumination. Uneven illumination can be very annoying; illumination of a sign face that falls off at the edges is more acceptable than light-dark-light stripes across the middle.

There is sometimes a conflict between the need of the designer for a slim box, and even illumination. If the fluorescent lamps are placed nearer the front face, patchy illumination will result. The temptation is then to put more lamps in the box, but this will increase the overall illumination and make the sign too bright. Over-bright signs may affect amenity, or in extreme cases, be a hazard to passing motorists. Acceptable brightness levels differ from country to country: in the UK, recommendations are made by the Institution of Lighting Engineers. Reducing sign brightness may be achieved by increasing the density of the front face material, fitting dimming equipment to the lamps, or illuminating the sign with cold-cathode lamps, which may be operated at a low current.

Halation
If the light source or the face of a sign is excessively bright, 'irradiation' or 'halation' will cause the individual letters to merge with their neighbours, if they are translucent against

an opaque background. The message disappears as a blur of light. If the letters are opaque against a translucent background, halation will cause them to be eroded in thickness until they virtually disappear, or lose much of the legibility for which they were designed.

Fluorescent lamps are also suitable for feature-lighting some essentially two-dimensional signs. If texture is an important aspect of the design, however, this method is unsuitable. Fluorescent light can sometimes be used for 'edge-lighting' glass and acrylic, often with the design etched into the front surface of the material.

Fluorescent lamps and the equipment required to control them are more expensive than incandescent lamps, but the overall running costs per lumen (unit of light energy) are much lower, because of their higher efficiency, so as a package, fluorescent lamps are cheaper. They can have more distribution at the blue, green and yellow end of the spectrum, making the colour rendering of the surface of the sign appear relatively cooler than under incandescent light. However, fluorescent lamps with improved colour rendering are becoming increasingly common. The quality of fluorescent light degrades over time, and may be different from tube to tube resulting in an uneven appearance. Tube maintenance and replacement should therefore be diligently managed.

Incandescent light

Incandescent lamps work by the application of electrical energy to a thin wire filament which starts to glow as it heats up. This is called incandescence. Thomas Edison is credited with the first practical incandescent lamp, which was lit on 19 October 1879. It was the first electric light source to be commercially available. Incandescent lamps – common light bulbs – are more popular than all other types; they have been available for longer, and people tend to prefer their colour distribution, which is towards the red end of the spectrum.

Tungsten filament
The wire filament that receives the electric current is normally tungsten. Tungsten lamps typically have a filament life of 1,000 hours. However, the efficiency, or more properly, efficacy, of an incandescent lamp in converting electrical energy to light energy is low and the life relatively short. Tungsten evaporates from the filament and is deposited on the inside of the glass bulb, making the lumen maintenance relatively poor. Both life and maintenance may be improved by using tungsten-halogen lamps, where the 'halogen cycle' tends to ensure the evaporated tungsten is deposited back on to the filament. Tungsten lamps produce a considerable amount of infra-red or heat radiation which may damage certain materials located near them. Also, they have a poor light output at the blue end of the visible spectrum.

◀ Fascia panels and hanging signs are often internally illuminated. In London, Digital has carefully positioned this sign in its main reception area, clearly announcing its presence.

▼ This splendid sign on Broadway, New York, is framed with a traditional light bulb border. The bulbs light up in sequence, attracting more attention to this massive display.

▼ The daytime aspect of illuminated signs should always be considered. Although high-up on this building, the Cats sign looks less than attractive during daylight hours.

▶ Ed's Easy Diner, in London's Soho district, is Britain's first American-style counter diner. Conceived and executed by Design House, it is an exercise in 50s nostalgia. The cold-cathode rocket motif and lettering are ingeneously authentic.

Light bulb signs use light bulbs in patterns – to enhance architectural features, for example, or forming a matrix to create a sign. This is perhaps the most common use of tungsten lamps in signing. Light bulbs are popular and eye catching, and are also commonly used for theatre frontages and for circus and fairground signs. Naturally, these signs are particularly effective at night. In bright sunlight, 'washout' occurs with coated lamps (pearl and coloured), but clear lamps allow filaments to compete effectively with sunlight.

Reflector lamps

Because of its compact nature, the light from the filament of an incandescent lamp may be accurately focused by means of a reflector, which may be an integral part of the lamp. Such lamps are particularly useful for feature and display lighting, and they can also enhance the effectiveness of outdoor message displays.

Internally silvered lamps (ISL) are internally silvered on the glass surface behind the filament, and may have a diffuser coating or 'frosting' on the front of the lamp. The degree of frosting determines whether it will be a spotlight or a floodlight.

Ellipsoidal reflector (ER) lamps have an ellipsoidal reflector behind the filament such that the beam has two focal points, one at the filament and the other 50 mm in front of the lamp. This lamp was developed to function efficiently in deep, recessed

fittings. It is uncommon in the UK.

Parabolic aluminized reflector (PAR) lamps have a parabolic reflector behind the filament focusing the light to give 50 per cent more directional light in spot and 300 per cent more in flood than comparable ISL lamps. Fittings for PAR lamps are large and conspicious. Because they are made from 'hard' glass, they may be safely used outside, without danger of the lamp shattering due to thermal shock in rain storms. There is an extremely wide range of types and sizes of PAR lamp, from very narrow spotlights to very wide floodlights, and there is a seemingly infinite variety of fixtures for them. They can be dimmed, filtered and softened, and their beams can be controlled by a variety of devices, including specially-cut masks that can precisely frame a sign.

Low-voltage halogen lamps
High-intensity, low-voltage tungsten-

halogen reflector lamps have become available fairly recently. The construction consists of a miniature tungsten-halogen lamp cemented into a reflector. Low-voltage incandescent lamps operate at 2 or 24 volts and need to be supplied from special low-voltage circuits or transformers. Suppliers of these systems claim that energy savings quickly compensate for the high cost of the lamps and fixtures. The lamps have a life of between 2000 and 4000 hours.

The shape and facet of the integral, internal reflectors of low-voltage lamps determine the angle of the beam. Their small size has led to the manufacture of numerous compact fittings, which are easily recessed or concealed in shallow ceiling cavities.

Mains-voltage halogen
Mains halogen lamps are far more efficient than ordinary tungsten

lamps. They maintain 95 per cent of their rated output at the end of their life, compared with 80 per cent for conventional tungsten lamps. Colour rendering can be excellent, and their expected life is between 2000 and 4000 hours.

High-intensity discharge (HID) lamps

HID lamps have been in use since the early 1930s, but the most exciting advances have been made in the last ten years. These lamps are very energy-efficient.

HID lamps produce light by means of a high-pressure electric arc discharge between electrodes, in an atmosphere of various gas vapours. Like incandescent lamps the filament or arc is compact enough to be controlled optically with reflectors, housings, lenses and so on. There are disadvantages however: unfamiliar colour rendering, making

normal tones take on a bluish-greenish cast; the 'warm up' and 'cool down' time needed; and the starter gear requirement.

Metal-halide lamps have good colour rendering properties, a life expectancy of 7,500 to 15,000 hours, and very high energy efficiency. A metal halide lamp gives 80-90 lumens/watt compared with 10-20 lumens/watt for an incandescent lamp.

Mercury lamps are about half as efficient as metal-halides, but have an extraordinarily long life of 24,000 hours, almost twice that of fluorescents. These lamps are generally used outdoors.

High pressure sodium lamps are the most efficient lamps available. They have a long life and good lumen maintenance, but unfortunately their monochromatic light makes everything look grey/brown. It is

these lamps that give British cities their familiar orange glow.

Cold-cathode and neon

Cold-cathode lamps are so called because they obtain their electrons for conduction by 'secondary emission' from a cold cathode. They tend to operate at higher voltages and lower currents than fluorescent lamps, but the principles are the same. Both rely on an ionized gas such as neon or argon to conduct electricity and emit illumination. A step-up transformer generates the high voltage required. Cold-cathode lamps may be dimmed and turned on and off rapidly, without detriment to their life.

The best-known cold-cathode lamps are the so-called 'neon lights' developed by the Frenchman George Claude in 1910. They had their first vogue in America in the 20s and 30s as a flamboyant style of outdoor

advertising. At first only two colours were available: red tubes filled with neon and blue with argon. The term 'neon' is often incorrectly used to describe all cold-cathode lamps. By 1939, when wartime restrictions were imposed, neon had become widely used all over the world for signs and general advertising purposes. In postwar years argon was used with fluorescent powder coatings inside the tube to achieve white and coloured light.

Cold-cathode is a popular choice for illuminated signing, as the tubing can be formed to follow accurately the shape of letters and designs. It is currently a favourite in Europe, reflecting the interest in American 50s and pastiche design. It is also enjoying a reunion with architecture, where it is used to accentuate

building contours, and it is an increasing feature of interior and point-of-sale signs. Additionally, 'neon sculptures' are now an acknowledged art form.

Today, only neon gas is in widespread use for a red colour. All the other colours are created by an argon (or neon/argon) gas discharge with mercury vapour providing ultraviolet light. A phosphor coating absorbs the ultraviolet and emits light of a certain colour. It is possible to modify colours by using coloured tubing.

Modern cold-cathode signs typically last 20-25,000 hours, or over two years of continuous operation. The eventual loss of performance is due to the depositing of mercury and other impurities on to the internal

▲ Richard Roger's out-of-town shopping centres for France's Usines chain of malls have attracted much attention. Here, in the Nantes centre, an indoor café uses cold-cathode lettering as a backdrop, complementing the high-tech image.

▶ This sign is a combination of cold-cathode tubing with a painted, patterned, background. The combination and contrast of the two elements create an unusual and sympathetic sign.

surface of the tube, causing progressive loss of light output. Tubes are generally replaced, not repumped. Maintenance, inspection and cleaning of the glass are important for safety and in detecting loose cables or poor power connections.

Manufacture

Cold-cathode signs are hand-made by highly skilled signmakers. Each sign is unique. A sign is made in sections, each with electrodes at either end, which are joined together at the back face, forming a 'continuous' tube. A pattern, of the shape of the section, is prepared on a paper sheet. This is drawn in reverse, so that all the joins are made behind the readable portion of the tubing (the face of the sign). The tubing is usually 11 mm, 15 mm, or 20 mm in diameter and may or may not have an

integral phosphor coating. The section of tubing to be bent is first heated over a low-intensity flame. As the glass begins to soften, the bend is carefully made to conform to the prepared pattern, and air is blown into the tube, making the diameter of the bend uniform with the rest of the tube.

Once the tubing is bent, and the sections and electrodes joined, the tube is ready to be pumped. In this process the tubing, phosphor coating and electrodes have to be heated to a temperature sufficient to release all the impurities. These impurities, together with the air in the tube, are removed by a vacuum system on the pump. When this operation is completed, the gas is introduced at a precise low pressure, together with the mercury.

▲ This well-mannered sign in a small London street quietly and appropriately identifies The Production Company through the use of a simple cold-cathode hanging sign. It does not attempt to compete visually with the strong surrounding environment.

◄ Larry's Chilli Dog sign by Robert Landau is a witty, fun piece of cold-cathode illumination, absolutely appropriate for the subject and the environment.

▼ The cast shadow of this Italian sign has repeated the word almost perfectly underneath the original, on the blind behind the glass. Although likely to be accidental in this instance, a designer may learn from such visual experiences.

Mounting

Skeleton letters can be connected to various frame structures, which are usually hung inside a window. Such frame structures include a self-contained metal frame with a bracket holding the transformer in the back of the unit; lighted glass tubing which can serve as a frame as well as part of the design; or, if the sign is not too intricate or fragile, a glass or metal rod which can be braced to the top of the sign.

In 'open front' lettering, the glass tube is mounted to the front of a metal-channel letter, closely following its shape. The metal-channel letter becomes the sign during the daytime and is virtually invisible at night, when it functions only to confine the light to the shape of the letter. In open-back or halo lettering, the tube is attached to the back of a letter with a solid metal front. The letters are mounted on supports away from the wall. At night, the lighted tubing illuminates the background, creating a silhouette of the sign. To disperse the light evenly the background is made of a light-coloured, non-reflective material.

Combination signs

For a better daylight effect, cold-cathode tubing is often used either as the internal illumination for legends with painted metal returns and self-coloured acrylic faces, or superimposed on painted metal legends. During daylight, when the tubes are switched off, the sign still provides a strong clear image. When used in conjunction with coloured surfaces, the colour of the cathode tubing has to be carefully chosen so as not to distort the paint colour.

Colour rendering

Colour can be determined according to certain systems, for example, the Colour Triangle, the Ostwald Colour System and the Munsell

Colour System. However, colour perception is not an exact science. Each individual's perception is subjective and different. So in practice when it comes to design decisions, the eye and the brain are the final judges.

Because of this subjectivity, decisions about colour schemes under the lighting conditions specified are best made *in situ*. Where the designer has little or no control over the ambient lighting this is essential.

When designing with colour there are two considerations. The first is the colour of the light itself. All sources of light have their own distinctive spectrum comprised of different intensities of colour bands or wavelengths of light; they may be stronger in blue, weaker in green, very short on red, or any possible combination. The second is the effect the light has on an object's colour appearance, its 'colour rendering'. The major factors affecting colour rendering are the colour and temperature of the light, and the colour and reflectivity of the object.

Colour measurement

Colour temperature may be measured in Kelvin (K), the absolute temperature scale, which is equal to degrees Celsius plus 273. The higher the Kelvin number, the more blue the light becomes, giving it a cooler appearance. There are two sources described for artificial daylight, which have the approximate temperatures of 5000K for noonday sunlight and 6500K for northern daylight.

Fluorescent lamps are rated in terms of their 'correlated' colour temperature. A colour-rendering index, expressed as a percentage, gives the designer the information needed to make design choices. When specifying fluorescent lamps for signs, designers should specify a colour-rendering index above 95 per cent.

▼ Split-flap message systems are commonly used in transportational environments – this one is in Waterloo Station, London. The station supplements the system by LRD displays, allowing non-standard messages to be conveyed as well as standard ones.

Reflection

The light we see, when looking at an object, is always reflected light. Nothing is visible until light hits its surface and is then reflected off it. The reflectivity of a surface depends on the type of material and its colour; a shiny white tile reflects more light than matt black paint. Surface reflectivity also influences how bright the surface appears to be; this is quantified as 'luminance' . Any brightness greater than the level that the eye is adapted to is known as 'glare'.

Direct glare

Glare is sometimes caused by experiencing an extreme range of brightness between two spaces, such as walking out of a darkened room into bright sunshine. A similar discomfort and reduction of vision will occur when an extreme range appears within a person's field of vision, for example when bright sunshine or daylight enters through a window next to a sign. As the eye adjusts to the light source it becomes less acute in perceiving the detail in the sign. This is similar to looking at a bare light source in a relatively dark place.

If glare is likely to be a problem with a sign, lights and reflective surfaces should be placed as carefully as possible on plan and adjusted as necessary once on site. Light will always be reflected from glossy surfaces at an angle equal to that of its approach or incidence. This is particularly important for signs which are externally illuminated by floodlights which are mounted above the sign.

Shadows

Shadows are part of the effect of light. They occur when an obstacle is placed in the path of light, because light travels in straight lines and cannot bend. If an object is illuminated so that it casts a shadow, the light reveals the object, and the shadow will provide additional information about its size, shape and spatial position. Binocular vision, which enables the perception of depth, combined with experience of the environment provides the majority of the information on size and shape.

Shadows have two qualities that can be controlled. The first is direction or angle; objects tend to be more pleasing when their shadows come from light directed at a 45°-60° angle. The second is the shadow's depth or density. The sun, with its parallel rays, gives the deepest and sharpest shadows. Of the artificial light sources, lamps with clear bulbs and tiny filaments, and fittings using projector lenses, give the deepest shadows. The softest shadows come from indirect or bounced light, from fluorescent lamps, from fittings that employ diffusers, and from pearlized lamps with long filaments. Distance is also a factor: the closer the object to the shadowed surface, the sharper the shadow.

Flat lighting

Flat light is the term used to describe light with minimal shadows, such as that of a completely cloudy, overcast day. Often objects appear dull and unexciting.

Measuring light

Illumination is a measure of the light falling on a surface and is expressed in terms of lumens per square metre (lux) or, previously, lumens per square foot (footcandles). Since there are approximately 10 square feet in a square metre, 10 lux is approximately equal to 1 footcandle.

Although illumination of a sign can be measured in this way, it is usually more important to know the brightness of the sign surface, or luminance. This, combined with the size of the illuminated sign face, will determine the effect a sign will have on its surroundings. For example, a large sign face which is excessively bright may be out of place in a quiet suburban neighbourhood, in extreme cases presenting a traffic hazard. Sign luminance is expressed in the metric term candelas per square metre. Photometers are available to measure both incident light (illumination) and transmitted light (luminance).

◄ In the Young Designers department of Harrod's, London, designed by Maurice Broughton Associates, white panels and columns define the space. Lighting from track-mounted and ceiling-recessed halogen sources, controlled by computer, is used to create this atmospheric signing.

Power needs

When planning the lighting for a sign the necessary electrical power must be estimated. If the sign is to go in an existing building the designer will require the building's electrical plans. In a proposed building, the designer should work with the architects, and must provide power where it is needed. Advice may always be sought from the sign manufacturer and the installation electricians.

Maintenance

Maintenance, as mentioned in Chapter 2, is an essential part of any illuminated sign. Good maintenance ensures that the sign will continue to operate in a safe and efficient manner. The accumulation of dirt and consequent loss of illumination over the life of lamps can reduce the level of light by as much as 50 per cent. Apart from cleaning and painting, the normal maintenance procedures include replacing incan-

descent lamps as soon as they burn out and replacing all fluorescent lamps at the end of their rated life. If a large number of lamps are required to light a sign or a sign system, the number of different types of lamps and rating should be kept to a minimum. This will lower the replacement-lamp inventory and relamping labour costs.

Electronic systems

Electronic signs respond to remote-control programming via a computer terminal. They are very much informational tools. Such signs are commonly used to attract attention to a building, a window, or a space within an environment. Electronic signs may be used to advertise a football score, the temperature, the time, opening hours, special offers, news headlines, train and aeroplane departure and arrival times, or even the increasing national debt!

▼ This incredible informational sign enables visitors to Times Square to watch the US national debt increase before their very eyes, using electronic means to alter the numerals.

Electronically controlled incandescent lamp matrix

Electronically controlled matrix signs employing incandescent lamps are probably more popular than any other electronic sign type. In the standard interchangeable message display, individual 7-lamp by 5-lamp modules, each capable of showing a letter or number, are placed side by side to produce a complete message. With a moving message unit, a continuous display may be seven lamps high and several hundred long. A lamp matrix, which is instructed by a control unit, may be extended horizontally and vertically, allowing several lines of message or large characters to be shown.

Computer-controlled cold-cathode

Computer controlled cold-cathode

signs provide the extraordinary and exciting signs of Las Vegas, Times Square and Piccadilly Circus. Although only appropriate in a small number of places, such signs are an important category of computer-controlled electronic signs.

Light-emitting diodes (LEDs)

Light-emitting diode displays are normally red, single-line, low-cost displays. They are typically found in shop-windows, airports and other locations where the information is viewed from relatively short distances. Character size is best kept to below five inches in height as larger signs tend to be less attractive and generate too much light, making the information difficult to read. Generally, LED displays have a low light output and are therefore suitable for interior use, although devices with intensities suitable for outdoor applications are now available. Green

▲ This assertive sign is by Jenny Holzer, a controversial New York artist whose work often takes the form of signs. Electrical signs such as this unusually large LED message have made her name.

and amber LEDs are alternatives to red. Indeed, multicoloured LED signs with large pictorial displays are now being produced.

Liquid-crystal displays (LCDs)

Liquid-crystal displays have found recent application in the signing industry. Previously LCD displays were restricted to very small areas such as digital readouts on calculators, watches and scientific instruments. Now LCD signs are being used at railways and airports. Character sizes over 100 mm are available, but there are still developmental difficulties with the much larger displays.

LCD displays may be purely reflective for their effect, depending on the external light sources; or they may combine reflective properties with the ability to transmit light for daylight application. Such 'transflective' displays can also be internally illuminated for night viewing.

A good range of colours can be used through the introduction of filters, and it is also possible to form a continuous matrix from LCD modules. However, LCD displays have relatively poor contrast compared with other display systems, as well as a limited viewing angle.

Light-reflecting displays (LRDs)

Light-reflecting displays have been available for many years, and are commonly seen in the UK in petrol stations. The system is electromagnetic; a segmented coloured disc aligns itself in response to a pulsed coil which generates a magnetic field, showing either a black or coloured face. LRD displays are available in a selection of colours and formats. Unlike other types of electronic displays, light-reflecting signs have very low power consumption. Power is not used to maintain the display, it is only consumed when the message changes.

▲ The world-famous British lawn tennis championship held at Wimbledon now features this massive electro-mechanical LRD scoreboard, manufactured by NEI-FP Displays, Bristol, England.

Split-flap messages

Split-flap message systems work by rotating characters or words on a motor-driven disc containing thirty-two or sixty-four flaps for letters, fewer for individual words. The messages are electronically remote-controlled, and offer instant changeability from a central console. Such systems are used almost exclusively in transportation terminals to indicate arrival and departure times, destinations, and other quickly interchangeable information. The system must be protected if used outside.

Television systems

These forms of electronic signing are probably developing faster than any other; significant advances are likely to be made in the next few years.

Television monitors, commonly in the form of cathode-ray tubes (CRTs), usually form part of these communication systems. Computerized directory systems employ many features available through this technology, such as touch-sensitive screens and vocal instructions. Alternatively a central video-camera copy unit connected to remote television monitors can provide communication of any image, similar to the way in which a television station transmits images. Resolution of the image is directly related to the quality of the camera and monitor. This arrangement is commonly used in transportational facilities, such as airports and railway stations, to transmit continuously updated information.

One of the most impressive electronic signs is the very large and expensive colour television screen seen at major sports stadiums. This utilizes many thousands of small, single-colour light sources, each one replacing a single coloured dot of a conventional television screen. Such a sign is capable of producing pictures of high clarity which can be seen from a great distance.

▼ A Jenny Holzer text on the large-format Sony Jumbotron, equivalent to a massive television screen. Advances in the application of this technology are expected to continue apace.

▼ This sign, carved into the marble walls below the I.M. Pei pyramid, is one of the 830 specified for the Cour Napoleon and the exterior of the Louvre alone, in the system designed by Kenneth Carbone for the Grand Louvre, Paris.

5 Materials and techniques

5 Materials and techniques

▶ Screenprinted fabric can provide a flexible means of signing for temporary schemes, such as this distinctive banner advertising real estate, designed by Coco Raynes, .

Increasingly wide choices of materials and techniques are used in signmaking and manufacturing. Technology has encouraged the development of numerous types of plastics, and new methods of fabrication and finish for many materials. Added to this, there is a resurgence in the use of the more traditional materials, including wood and stone.

The right choice of materials is often complicated. There is an enormous range from which to choose, and decisions may be based on any number and combination of factors: cost, appearance, durability, wind loading, resistance to vandalism, maintenance and so on. The choice of materials is also fundamental to the successful implementation of the design. The sign has to look and 'feel' right. In the words of William Noonan, director of the graphic design department at San Diego Zoo and Wild Animal Park, 'We think good graphic design really works when all the elements are in harmony. What most people see is the colour, texture, and shape. What they don't see is the designer assessing the options he [or she] has in the use of materials, fasteners, cements, and paints. The depth of beauty of the product is reflected in how wisely the materials are used.' Many designers are conservative in their use of material, and seem unaware of their lost creative opportunities. The potential of different materials, techniques and finishes is worth study, so that designers can make informed creative choices.

Common processes

The following processes are common to a number of materials. It is not an exhaustive list, but a section of the more popular techniques.

Screenprinting (silkscreening)
Screenprinting was developed from the ancient art of stencilling. Today, photographic stencils are used. The printing screen consists of a rigid frame, usually metal, over which a synthetic mesh fabric is stretched and adhered. Ink is poured on to one end of the screen and a squeegee is then used to draw it evenly across to the other end. As this takes place the slight pressure applied to the squeegee forces ink through the open areas of the mesh on to the material beneath. There is usually a separate screen for each ink colour. Perhaps the greatest advantage of the process is its ability to print on to a wide range of materials such as paper, board, wood, plastics, glass, ceramics, metals and textiles.

▲ The sign for Plaza 9, Oxford Street, London, is made from three-dimensional, transparent perspex letters on a mirrored background. It is a memorable sign which continually changes through its reflected distortions - eyecatching but not always easy to read.

Spray painting (foil cut and spray)

The traditional art of signwriting is the forerunner of the technique known as 'foil cut and spray', so called because the material to be decorated was masked using lead foil, and a stencil cut to leave an image which was then coloured in. After peeling away the foil, a background colour was applied. Foil has been superseded by other materials, such as plastic paint and rubber film, which dries, hardens and can be peeled away once the stencilled image has been spray-painted. This highly-skilled process tends to be used as an alternative to screenprinting for short runs and for unusually shaped signs.

Sandblasting

A mask or stencil (made of self-adhesive paper sheet, tape, or a rubber or plastic solution which hardens) absorbs the sand or abrasive particles which are blasted at the material. The image is made by abrasion of the unprotected area of the material. When the correct depth of image has been achieved, it may be highlighted using an appropriate 'filling' such as paint. Sandblasting is usually performed in a sealed or shielded compartment, when small signs are being produced. It may also be performed *in situ;* skilled operators are hard to find, however. Sandblasting is suitable for almost any material: plastic, metal, wood, glass, stone, brick, concrete and so on.

Casting

Casting is the process by which signs are formed from a mould. It is suitable for any material which may be poured into a mould and hardened. These include plastic, metal, glass, concrete and so on.

Extrusion

This is a method of forming mouldings by forcing a material through suitable dies.

Die-cutting

Many materials may be die-cut. This is the process of cutting the material using a pattern or template for the design.

Engraving

Plastic, wood, stone and other materials may be engraved by hand or by machine. Laser machines can be used very effectively to achieve precision engraving, although not all materials can be worked in this way.

Materials

Plastic, metal, wood, glass, stone, concrete, brick and ceramic are all suitable materials for signmaking, and the designer should be familiar not only with the substance itself, but also with its relevant properties, and with the fabrication processes appropriate to each material.

Plastics

Plastics are the most commonly used materials for making signs. In fact, the introduction of plastic sheet, after the Second World War, revolutionized the signing industry. It was stable, easily fabricated, capable of outdoor exposure and available in a wide range of colours. Its introduction deskilled the signmaking process and signs became gradually more affordable. Today, the choice of plastic materials from which to fabricate signs is vast.

Plastics are subject to temperature change, so the expansion co-efficients of the materials they are fixed to must be carefully considered. Inflexible fastening may result in sign breakage; large, flat, horizontal sheets will deform under continuous pressure or their own weight without antideflection studs.

Plastics which are used for signing include acrylic, polyvinyl chloride (PVC), polycarbonate, butyrate, styrene, polypropylene, glass-reinforced plastic (GRP), fibre-reinforced polyester-nylon, (FRP-Nylon) and vinyl.

Acrylic

Acrylic plastics can be colourless and transparent, or coloured to be opaque or translucent. Surfaces may be gloss or matt. Opaque acrylic maintains the most even and intense colour, and is commonly used in illuminated signs to hide the light source (see Chapter 4). Appropriate paints

▲ This exterior sign for the Museum of Contemporary Art, Los Angeles, was designed by Chermayeff and Geismar Associates. The stainless-steel plate has coloured acrylic 'punched through' from the back to form raised lettering. The front of the letter surface is stainless steel. At night this sign is illuminated through the acrylic.

fuse with the surface and become integral with it. Acrylics have good weather-resistance and fade little in sunlight.

Acrylics generally have low impact-strength and poor surface hardness unless treated with a hardcoat. Untreated, the surface tends to build up static electricity that attracts dust and dirt; some manufacturers provide special hardcoatings to eliminate this problem. Acrylics are highly flammable, although this property can be modified by the addition of a fire retardent. They can be thermoformed to produce almost any shaped sign 'pan', sawed, drilled and machined like a soft metal.

The two methods of producing acrylic sheet are casting and extrusion. Acrylic may also be combined with other chemicals, forming products with specific properties.

Cast acrylic sheet (CAS) is made by constructing a cell of two large separated sheets of glass. A thick syrup of methyl methacrylate monomer, containing a heat catalyst and all the necessary dyes and pigments, is poured into the cell. After removal from an oven, the glass sheets are split away and the CAS is protected by paper covers and trimmed to standard sizes. It is robust enough to withstand manufacture, transportation, installation and maintenance stresses. CAS is lightweight and self-supporting, making it ideal for large signs; it is extensively used out of doors.

Extruded acrylic sheet (EAS) is produced by heating a polymerized granular resin, polymethyl methacrylate (PMMA), until molten which is fed under pressure through an automatic extruding machine to emerge as continuous sheet. It is then cooled and cut to length. Because of this method of manufacture, how ever, EAS has a residual strain in the material. If subjected to paints, adhesives or solvents, this strain may be released in the form of surface crazing. EAS is easier to thermoform than CAS, it 'flows' more freely,

▶ Glass-reinforced plastic is a material associated by many with architectural panelling. Here, London's Design House has employed artist Gerda Rubinstein to use this versatile material for a stunning sculpture that is the focus of the main entrance to wine merchants South of the Bordeaux.

▼ Vinyl offers an extensive range of materials from which the designer may choose. Here, the Body Shop displays the effective use of vinyl for this fascia treatment in Oxford Street, London.

allowing improved definition. It is especially suitable for large-scale signing programmes, where long production runs make this automated process economically attractive.

Impact-modified acrylic is an acrylic with a rubber additive making it more flexible and impact-resistant than regular cast or extruded acrylic. At present this material can only be extruded. It is used where signs need extra protection. It does have certain disadvantages: poor weathering properties, a soft surface, poor tensile and rigidity strength, and a decrease in toughness with temperature – at 0°C it is only as good as regular acrylic.

PVC
There are two types of PVC – rigid and foam; the two products are quite different from each other and each is particularly suitable for specific signs and environments.

Rigid PVC can be made in the same way as acrylic, but it is adversely affected by sunlight, and does not have the same excellent 'memory' when formed. Although less flammable than acrylic, it can generate poisonous fumes in the presence of external flames. It tends to be more vandal-resistant and less expensive than acrylic. Rigid PVC is suitable for non-illuminated, low-level signing which is likely to be damaged, such as car-park signing. It is also used in locations where moisture resistance is critical.

Foam PVC is a strong, lightweight, opaque, honeycombed material which can be vacuum-formed, locally bent and welded. It is available in a limited range of standard colours. Problems include expansion through heat absorption, such as the heat from a light source. This material is only ever used in internal, non-illuminated situations, such as point-of-sale (POS) and in-store displays and exhibition stands.

Polycarbonate
Polycarbonate is an extremely tough material, enjoying the properties of acrylic with the advantage of being virtually shatterproof. A bullet will pass through leaving only a burnt hole; thicker sheets will even stop a bullet. Due to its high heat-distortion resistance, polycarbonate has excellent fire-resisting properties. However, it has poor weatherability and is likely to yellow within five years of installation. It is susceptible to atmospheric erosion and is sensitive to naturally occuring radiation.

A 10 per cent light transmission loss in ten years is not uncommon. Its surface is easily scratched.

Polycarbonate comes in a limited range of colours and can also be clear. It can be supplied in rolls, and therefore in much greater lengths and widths than acrylic. It is commonly used in enclosed public areas, such as banks, building societies and sports stadiums, affording protection as well as a clear view. It is also used for illuminated signs where vandalism is a problem.

Butyrate
Butyrate plastic is optically clear, impact-resistant and easily formable. It is available in a limited range of translucent and transparent colours, and is especially adaptable for vacuum-forming.

Styrene
Styrene is too brittle for exterior use, yellows rapidly and affords minimum light transmission. It is a cheap material which may be vacuum-or press-formed; it is available in several grades, giving extra durability, impact resistance and viscosity. The material is however, highly flammable, fragile if mishandled and difficult to clean. Styrene is commonly used for internal display, POS signs, and signs that are laminated to awkward places.

Polypropylene
More appropriate for signing than styrene, this plastic is not as well suited to exterior use as acrylic. It is more flexible and therefore has a tendency to 'throw off' letters of different materials which are not fused to its surface. It is available in milky white, black, and colours on a minimum order basis.

Glass-reinforced plastic (GRP)
Glass-reinforced plastic is a hard-wearing, lightweight laminate of glass and plastic. It is a high-impact material with light-diffusing ability and is commonly used for fascia panels and projecting signs.

Fibre-reinforced polyester nylon (FRP-Nylon)
This is an inexpensive, relatively thin, flexible plastic product. It has a noticeable surface texture and

grain. It must be fixed to a flat surface for support, and special attention needs to be paid to handling and drying.

Flexible vinyl or nylon-reinforced vinyl

Flexible vinyl is a three-layer composite material. A woven mesh of polyester yarn or 'scrim' forms the central element, a clear PVC resin is applied to the underside and an opaque white PVC (with UV stabilizers, antifungicides and light absorbers) is applied to the top display surface. There are three main ways of applying graphics to this material: screenprinting, using pressure-sensitive film and using dry colour transfer.

Flexible vinyl is an alternative to rigid plastics, and is used for many back-illuminated signs, especially when sign dimensions exceed rigid sheet sizes. Translucent, flexible vinyl is tensioned using a frame system giving a flat, lightweight, evenly illuminated sign with no light leakage. Some manufacturers provide a warranty against the sign 'blowing out' in high winds. The frame system is commonly used for very long signs, such as petrol-station canopies. It may also be used for unusually shaped signs, where the vinyl can be wrapped around a supporting frame.

Adhesive film

Adhesive films usually consist of extremely thin vinyl or other plastic with adhesive backings, which can provide either permanent or removable messages printed on the front surface. Letters and symbols may be formed by 'punching' through the different types of films, with either steel rules or thermal dies. These signs can be applied to any suitable smooth surface, and there is a wide range of colours resistant to UV fading. Translucent and opaque film may be used for external and internal applications, window and display graphics and vehicle livery. Reflective vinyls, once exclusively used for road traffic signs, are now increasingly being applied to commercial signs and for vehicle livery.

Computer-aided design and manufacture (CAD/CAM) have had a massive impact on the popularity of this material, producing a precise, high-quality finish. A CAD/CAM machine will carry a standard set of typefaces, which may be manipulated by the operator. Designs and logos are scanned from camera-ready artwork and treated as standard items. Text and graphic images may be merged on screen and in many cases a full-colour copy of the final design is provided for client approval.

Transfers and decals use adhesive film to produce their effects. Transfer letters are letters printed in vinyl ink on the back of a carrier sheet. Individual letters are optically spaced and rubbed on to the sign surface, by burnishing; protective coatings are sometimes recommended. However, lacquer-based products will yellow. Transfer letters can be purchased as stock items, and custom alphabets can also be ordered.

Decals are images printed on the face-side of an adhesive vinyl film. The two major categories are pressure-sensitive and water-activated markings. Decals enable signs to be applied to unusually shaped smooth surfaces, such as oil-trucks and aeroplanes.

Coloured plastics

Plastics may be coloured by spray painting, silkscreening or integral pigment. Some silkscreen inks, especially designed for use on acrylics, contain solvents which soften and etch the surface to provide a good key.

Some vinyl-process paste inks penetrate the film slightly and produce a similar effect. When coated with a clear lacquer, these colours become virtually permanent. Pigmented plastics are supplied from manufacturers in a wide variety of colours. Although expensive, they are the most permanent form of coloured plastic.

A matt finish applied to plastic will reduce the problems of glare and

◀ This window display, advertising the Andy Warhol retrospective exhibition at the Museum of Modern Art, New York, is a terrific example of an intelligently designed and accurately applied adhesive film sign. The repeat pattern and use of colour refer to the artist's work.

reflection. However, this finish may cause copy to become fuzzed, if the copy is on the reverse of plastics over 1/8 in. thick.

Plastic laminates
Lamination is the process by which different materials are layered and bonded together. Certain laminates are particularly suitable for signs.

Laminated acrylics can be fabricated like wood or soft metal. They are used almost exclusively for engraving, and are inappropriate for moulding or vacuum-forming.

Laminated fibreglass is often used to add bulk to a sign; the fibreglass face is laminated to plywood, honeycomb cardboard, other plastic or polyurethane foam. Integral-colour fibreglass layers can be bonded to one or both sides of the sheet. These signs have a virtually unlimited life outdoors.

Protective laminates are protective plastic surfaces that can be bonded to core materials such as plywood, particle board and metal. These plastic surfaces are manufactured in different grades for vertical and horizontal surfaces; the back is sanded to maintain a uniform thickness and to facilitate bonding. They are only ever used in interiors. A variety of colours and finishes is available.

Plastic processes
There are a number of processes in which plastics can be manipulated to form signs.

Vacuum-forming is a process in which heated plastic is clamped directly on to the edges of a mould and sucked into it by air pressure. The plastic can be stretched to various sizes, depending on the thickness of the sheet and the amount of heat. This process is commonly used for large signs as it gives strength and durability to the form. It tends to produce signs which have rounded edges.

Moulding is a very similar process to vacuum-forming and is sometimes used in conjunction with it, for improved definition. A heated sheet of plastic is pressed between two moulds.

Casting is a cheap process used to mass-produce small letters. Silicone rubber moulds are filled with polyester which are then allowed to cure, or dry out. These letters are primarily for use on bulletin boards.

Die-cutting is a process only used when large numbers of signs are required.

Engraving of plastics can be done by hand or machine. Hand-engraving is unusual. Machine-engraving involves a two-colour, laminated sandwich called 'engraving stock' (ES) plastic. The image is cut through a coloured layer to expose a contrasting inner core. Engraving is frequently used for small signs.

Embedding is used to 'embed' messages in plastic. Messages may be on a substrate (usually silkscreened paper or vinyl), which is

◀ Pentagram designers John McConnell and Ralph Selby produced these superb sheet-steel arrows for the London Docklands Development Corporation, coating them with resin to improve their resistance to corrosion. The construction technique was inspired by the shipbuilding which once flourished in the area.

▶ Henrion Ludlow & Schmidt's sign system for the London Docklands Corporation includes these dramatic signs, which capture a suitably nautical element while giving clear directions.

then flooded with polyester resin. Messages may also be 'integral'; the messages are printed on the underside of the plastic. A polyester gel coat is used as the background colour, and the sign is reinforced with glassfibre. The resulting panels are often sandwiched over a core material of honeycomb cardboard, plywood or high-density polyurethane foam. A polyurethane coat has better abrasion, impact- and moisture-resistance and flexural strength than a polyester coat.

Metals

Metals are the second most common materials used for signmaking. The metals most frequently in use are steel and aluminium; although steel is often used due to its strength and cost advantages, the trend, particularly in America, is towards an increasing use of aluminium.

Steel
In the UK, there is still a large market for individual letter signs, which are made of steel because of the ease of fabrication. Steel must always be treated in some way to improve its corrosion resistance; the method of treatment is usually defined by the use of the sign.

Lead-coated mild sheet steel is one of the most traditional metals used in the sign industry. It can be soldered, but in the cleaning process the lead coating is removed and has to be replaced. It is commonly used for built-up letters.

Zinc-coated mild sheet steel is produced by applying a zinc protective coating by an electrolytic process. Over the life of a sign, the zinc gives sacrificial protection to the steel, limiting corrosion 'creep'. The zinc coating is very thin and is primarily used for indoor applications (such as refrigerator bodies); hot-dipped zinc is much thicker and is suitable for outdoor signing applications.

Both lead and zinc provide protection for the steel surface, but cannot protect cut edges. Any paint used on lead- and zinc-coated steel needs to be selected with care. It must promote adhesion and be compatible with the metallic coating.

Stainless steel is an expensive and prestigious material. It has high corrosion resistance. The presence of chromium gives it the unique ability to 'self repair' if mechanically damaged. Small additions of nickel and molybdenum significantly increase corrosion resistance. Stainless steel is available in a wide range of colours and finishes.

Descaled stainless steel has a 'mill' or untreated finish and is much cheaper than stainless steel. It is easier to work with and is often preferred where appearance is not the prime factor, as, for example, in the backing panel for a fascia sign. This is a first-class material for signs which are then painted. It is widely used in the UK.

Structural steel is commonly used to support by freestanding signs. Rolled hollow and circular hollow sections provide a 'finished face', and as such tend to be used where the sign is completely exposed.

Vitreous enamelled metal is glass fused to a metal substrate and forming a hard smooth coating. The coating itself is then fused at around 870°C to produce a unique permanent finish which has a life expectancy of around thirty years. In the UK, signs are commonly made of vitreous enamelled steel, or engraved bronze infilled with vitreous enamel and fused. Messages may be applied by silkscreen, offset printing, water-slide transfer, or partial removal of the second enamel coat. Colours can be bright and vibrant, and most British Standard and Pantone colours may be matched.

Enamel is a very hard material which has outstanding resistance to chemicals and heat. It is ideal in hostile environments. However, as the surface is effectively glass, it will chip and crack, especially if the expansion and contraction of the metal is excessive. This material is used for flush and built-up lettering, street nameplates, bus stops and many demanding applications.

Aluminium

The principal qualities of aluminium are lightness, good strength-to-weight ratio and excellent durability. It is non-combustible, non-toxic and highly resistant to chemical corrosion. Aluminium can be alloyed with various other metals to obtain desirable properties and characteristics. It can be produced in sheets, extruded, wrought and cast. It can also be manipulated and formed with ease. One of the few disadvantages of aluminium is that it is difficult to join to itself and other materials other than by riveting or screwing.

The choice of the correct grade of aluminium and the forming process used for making a sign can be complicated. Manufacturers ask designers to seek their advice at design stage. Often designers do not exploit the wealth of information and advice offered by signmakers and manufacturers.

Aluminium sheet is a popular material for making signs; it comes in many different grades and surface finishes.

Extruded aluminium is an accurately dimensioned length of an aluminium alloy of predetermined shape, which is produced by forcing semi-molten metal through a die. The material is then straightened, cut to length and loaded into ovens for heat treatment or annealing. Aluminium extrusions are commonly used to produce road signs and signs for shopfronts and petrol stations. Other typical applications include in-store displays, billboards and electronic display boards. Aluminium castings are not normally used in sign manufacture.

Aluminium finishes

Aluminium may be finished in a variety of ways, including mill finishing, painting, anodizing, PVC-lamination, polishing and embossing.

Mill finish, the untreated metal finish, will, if left, form a natural oxide layer on its surface which acts as a barrier against atmospheric corrosion.

Painting is the most common finish for aluminium. A strong-etch primer is needed to cut into the surface oxide layer and provide a good key for the paint.

Aluminium extrusions are immersed in a tank of water-based acrylic paint (available colours at present are only white and bronze). They are positively charged, attracting the negatively charged paint, which forms the paint layer. This process gives a uniform paint thickness and is efficient and reliable. The size of signs is limited by the size of the paint tank.

After pre-treatment, aluminium extrusions pass through an automatic powder-spraying booth where they are electrostatically sprayed with polyester or epoxy paint. There can be problems with inconsistent thickness and variations in colour, paint build-up in tight tolerance areas, and 'orange peel' effect.

Anodizing, which is commercially unique to aluminium, is an electrolytic process that provides a dense, chemically inert, protective aluminium oxide layer, which is an integral part of the underlying metal. It cannot peel or flake. Most anodized films are translucent and many colours and special effects are attainable. Hard anodizing produces an especially dense and durable layer, but care should be taken to avoid a crazed surface.

Bronze and brass

Bronze and brass are alloys of copper and zinc, with traces of other metals in varying proportions. They can be cast from ingots, sawn from sheet metal or extruded. Bronze is a bright coppery-red colour. Casting ingots are generally an alloy of 85 per cent copper, 5 per cent lead, 5 per cent nickel and 5 per cent zinc. Red brass is 84-6 per cent copper and 14-16 per cent zinc, and yellow brass is 70 per cent copper and 30 per cent zinc. Their bright finishes can be preserved by lacquering, pre-oxidized by chemical attack, or left to oxidize naturally. Brass accepts chrome plating better than bronze.

Long-established as materials for signmaking, bronze and brass are associated with traditional institutions and values. The constant need for polishing, which undoubtedly caused their decline in popularity at one time, accounts for their association with care and constant attention to detail, qualities that may be desirable today.

Laminates

Very thin aluminium sheets are available for laminating to sign or display surfaces. The metal comes in strips, tiles or sheets, in a variety of finishes and any shade of anodization. It can be easily formed and glued. Aluminium also comes in laminated sheets with a polyethylene core. Other metal laminates can be bonded to a steel core, on a phenolic backing, and are recommended for flat vertical-surface applications. The metals available are copper, brass and chromium.

◄ The address of this office building really stands out on its distinctive stainless-steel identificational pillar. This wonderful material looks as good as new in a tough Manhattan environment.

◀ These beautiful bronze building plaques were spotted in Italy by Jim Bodoh. All delightfully different, they complement each other, with the constant size and fixing details providing visual consistency.

▼ Designer Takenobu Igarashi was the Art Director for this directory sign for Nippon Insurance Company in Toranomon, Tokyo. It is made from solid coloured aluminium, and 'fits' perfectly in this exterior setting.

▶ This dramatic picture shows a sign for Thorn EMI being made in a traditional signmaker's factory in London. The machine traces the outline of the letters from the original design and transfers the image in the required size, ready for engraving.

Metal processes

Common methods of sign fabrication include:

Cast metal letters are solid, one-piece signs or individual letterforms which are often used when durability or prestige identification is required. The casting process is carried out in three stages. A pattern is made, usually out of wood, metal or plastic, which is slightly larger than the finished sign, to allow for shrinkage of the metal as it cools. A 'rubbing' is made to 'prove' the pattern, allowing the designer to view the final result of the casting. A mould is prepared and molten metal is poured into it, allowed to cool and removed. Finishing methods include machining, polishing, plating, anodizing, enamelling and painting.

Sawn metal can be sawn by hand to make solid, often one-piece signs. These are commonly used whenever durable identification in low relief or unusual sign forms are desired.

Sheet-metal signs are hollow, thin-walled three-dimensional structures. They are made by hand. The sides and faces of the signs are usually flat and broad in area. Various sheet metals include stainless steel, copper and aluminium.

Die-stamped metal signs usually consist of individual letterforms stamped out of aluminium or stainless-steel sheet. Two dies are used in the process.

Die-embossing is very similar to die-stamping, but in this case the dies do not fit as closely together. This process produces signs from sheet metal that have a soft, rounded, low-relief dimensional surface. After embossing these signs are often enamelled or silkscreened. They are usually small whole signs, but sometimes individual letterforms are made this way. They are most often used as lightweight, inexpensive markers, where large numbers of low-cost durable signs are required.

Engraved metal signs are cut as a shallow, negative relief. Often the letters are filled with enamel. They are generally used for small identificational signs or dedication plaques. Engraving machines, lasers, sandblasters and routers can be used to engrave metal.

Photo-etched metal signs are thin plates that frequently have a large body of small or intricate design elements, in extremely shallow, negative relief. Camera-ready artwork is photographed to the desired size and a film positive made. The positive is placed over a metal plate which has been coated with light-sensitive gel. On exposure to a bright light source the areas of gel covered by the opaque part of the film remain soluble and are removed by running hot water. These unprotected areas are then etched out in an acid bath. Letterforms are often coloured or filled.

Anodized photo-sensitive aluminium plates and foils can embed any image, including half-tones, to give a sign which is virtually indestructible. The surface can be hardcoated to guarantee a twenty-five-year life in any weather conditions.

Wood

During the past five to ten years the widespread craft renaissance and the green revolution has meant a revival of all things traditional and hand-made. Wood is one of the oldest and most beautiful natural materials known to man. Its attraction stems from its colours, internal structure, unpredictability, strength, rigidity, smell, lightness and warmth. It is a favourite with many designers.

Wood can be worked and jointed easily, with relatively simple tools, allowing unusual forms and shapes

◀ This exquisite building in Chiang Mai, Thailand, has the most perfect hanging sign. The magnificent slab of natural wood has been carved with expressive sculptural Thai letters, and to read '6 Pole House', in English.

▶ Coco Raynes designed the complete visual identity for Loulou's bakery, in Boston, Massachusetts. The window letters are handcarved wood, finished with smart red, high-gloss, epoxy paint.

to be created. Its final appearance depends on the choice of wood and the state of the wood: the surface can be bark, rough cut, smooth and carved with applied finish or colour. Unlike many materials, the appearance of wood often improves with age.

For all practical purposes wood may be divided into two types, hardwood and softwood. Hardwoods are from deciduous trees and come mostly from the warmer climates of the temporate and tropical zones. Examples include mahogany, oak, teak, beech, maple and birch. They are generally more durable and more suitable for signing purposes. Naturally, however, designers will need to be sensitive to the environmental issues involved with the use of certain hardwoods, using only those which are in plentiful supply, and in no way encouraging the further destruction of rainforests. Softwoods are usually more appropriate for internal signs, and come from coniferous trees, including pine, fir, cedar, redwood, cypress and spruce.

Designers should be careful to choose a good piece of wood, free from knots and imperfections. Wood should always be protected from rot, decay and insect attack. Where it is to be used in large quantities, the flammability of the material needs to be considered.

Natural wood may be waxed or lacquered, stained, painted, bleached, burnished, applied as a veneer, and used in combination with other materials. It may be employed as a surface for printing, transfers and so on. Typically wood is used for built-up letters, fascias, and one-off signs which are carved and gilded.

Wooden signs are more common in the US than in the UK and Europe. Each different type of wood has its own particular characteristics.

Mahogany - Only a few types of this wood are suitable for exterior use. Lanuan is soft, open-grained, light to reddish-brown in colour, with fair finishing characteristics and dimensional stability. African Mahogany is medium-hard,

open-grained, light to dark reddish brown with excellent finishing and dimensional stability characteristics. Tropical American Mahogany or Honduras Mahogany is medium-hard, open-grained, with excellent dimensional and finishing characteristics. It is a rich golden brown colour. Tanguile or dark Philippine Mahogany is an open-grained hardwood of medium hardness, good finish retention and poor dimensional stability.

White oak, plain-sawn, is a greyish tan, open-grained hardwood available in a wide range of patterns and colours. It has poor dimensional stability.

East Indian Teak is the most expensive wood available for signs, but it is extremely hard, has outstanding weatherability and is very dimensionally stable. The colour of this open-grained wood is tawny yellow to dark brown.

Pine is a close-grained softwood. Idaho and Sugar Pine are creamy white, Northern Pine is creamy white

to pink, Ponderosa Pine is light to medium pink. Yellow Pine or Short-leaf Pine is pale yellow and the only 'hard' pine, which is actually only of medium hardness.

Douglas Fir is a close-grained reddish tan wood, fir is available in two grains, flat and vertical. The vertical grain is more expensive, but has better stability than the flat, which tends to splinter and raise. It is a softwood with fair to good finishing characteristics and dimensional stability.

Red or Western Cedar is a soft, close-grained wood of light to dark red colour. It has a high natural decay resistance, as well as good finishing and dimensional stability characteristics.

Redwood is available in two grades: All-Heartwood, which is highly resistant to termites and decay, and Sapwood-Containing. It is deep red and excellent for exterior signing. It has outstanding weatherability, dimensional stability and takes finishes well. Clear All Heart V.G. is a special vertical grain selection, with exceptional weatherability, stability and finish retention.

Cypress is a close-grained wood with a slightly red to yellowish-brown natural colour. It has medium hardness and medium to high dimensional stability. It receives finishes well.

Wood-composite products

Certain wood composites can be used for signmaking. They tend to be more suitable for indoor signing since they are not usually very weatherproof.

Medium-density fibreboard is a composite product manufactured from natural wood fibre. Resins and other agents are added to bind it together, and it is then compressed into a dense sheet and sanded smooth. MDF has good stability and loadbearing strength, and may be printed on directly. However, it has to be sealed in humid conditions as it has a tendency to retain moisture and swell. It is typically used as a background fascia panel and in shopfitting displays.

Wood laminates

The most common laminated wood product used in signing is plywood. Standard ply can be made from virtually any wood. It is constructed by peeling thin layers of wood from a rotating log and gluing these together under extreme pressure and heat. In order to prepare the plywood for use as a sign face, care must be taken to fill and seal all flaws and edges before applying a finish.

Medium-density overlay (MDO) is made using a layer of phenolic resin-impregnated fibre sheet is bonded to both sides of the plywood. This covering eliminates the grain of the wood and effectively seals both major surfaces of the panel. Edges remain unprotected.

Metal-clad plywood is made by laminating metal to one or both sides of the plywood.

Wood processes

Common methods of sign fabrication from wood include:

Carving is a very traditional craft.

Letters may be chiselled by hand or cut by routing machines. These letters may be left in their natural state or filled with paint or epoxy. Reflective glass beads may be added to the paint/epoxy mixture, but these weather badly and soon lose their reflective qualities, as does reflective paint.

Sandblasting can be used to etch a design into wood with fine sand, using a rubber stencil. This process is only recommended for woods that have a very even grain, such as redwood, since the surface of other woods will splinter and the edges will be uneven.

Laser engraving is a technique used for making small wooden signs, usually pictorial in nature. The cutting of the laser beam is precise and very sharp.

Glass

Glass windows are usually the transparent barriers protecting internal signs. In retailing, signs seen on and through glass in the display window often supplement other signs further inside, bringing information within the normal field of vision of the passer-by. Independent signs may also be made of glass.

Glass can cause problems for a designer, such as reflections or possible show-through of undesired background. Additionally, the expansion co-efficients of different materials have to be carefully considered before their application to glass. Vinyl letters, which stretch, tend to be more appropriate than other individual letters. Some types of tinted glass are susceptible to crazing and cracking when used in direct sunlight. Where vandalism is a problem, plastic should be specified.

In spite of its drawbacks, glass is a beautiful and versatile material for making signs. It may be plain, coloured, transparent, opaque, mirrored and stained. It may also be used as a substrate material for paint, silk-screen ink, transfers and so on.

Glass processes

Processes for making signs from glass include acid-etching, sandblasting, brilliant glass-cutting and gilding. Naturally, the application of lettering and images to glass involves a degree of obscuration.

Acid etching is used to ornament glass in any shape with the most elaborate designs of lines or dots. Etching produces a milky image accompanied by gradation of shade, and depth and strength of line. Hydrofluoric acid is used; the exact concentration of the acid is sometimes referred to as the 'recipe' and is a secret handed down through family generations.

The design may be pricked or 'pounced' directly on to the glass, or

◀ Medium-density fibreboard has been used here in the construction of wallside canopies for the Asda store in Taunton, England. These panels have a flat, smooth surface, free of the usual grains and knots found in natural wood, so they are ideal for screenprinted signs.

▶ Much magnificent glasswork is found in English public houses. Many are famous for their brilliant glass cutting, stained and etched glass. This window in the Cambridge Arms, Cambridge, is a fine example of the latter.

▼ The gilded letters of the Church of Jesus Christ of Latter-Day Saints, in London, have a certain prestige as well as a life and spirit due to the use of gold. The dappled light here intensifies the effect of the lettering.

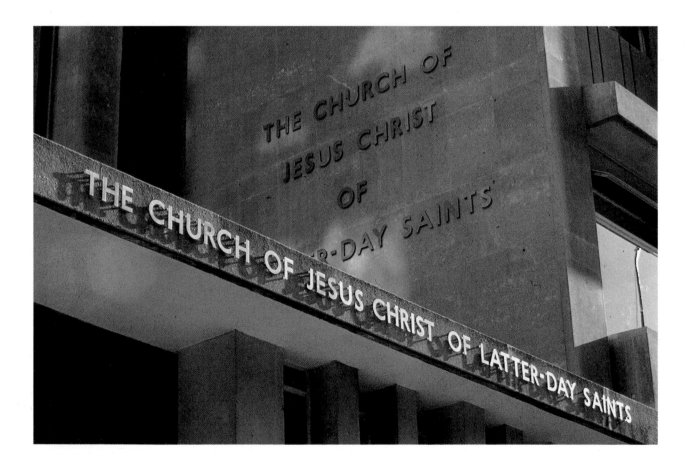

▼ Goddard and Gibbs Studios designed and made this backlit stained-glass mural for Austin Reed, Regent Street. The history of the store was used as a theme for the work. The deep blue, red and silver, together with the subtle colours achievable with hand-made glass, make a striking impact.

on to tracing-paper used as a guide. The ground, or acid-resisting mixture, is painted on to the glass (following the design), leaving the image area free. Acid is then poured on to the glass for the required amount of time. This process is repeated until the design is completed.

It is also possible to etch glass *in situ* by silkscreening an image with an etching compound, and washing it off quickly when the desired depth has been reached.

At first sight there is little difference between etched and sandblasted glass. But sandblasted glass has a coarser, more granular effect than etched glass, and consequently produces a greyer, weaker image. Both processes may be accompanied by brilliant glass-cutting.

Brilliant glass cutting is a traditional skill requiring many years of experience. Designs are worked by lowering a glass sheet, which is suspended in a counterbalanced cradle, on to a cutting wheel of willow wood. The cut is fed with water and sometimes an abrasive. It is, of course, impossible to correct a mistake. Letters can be shaped which are more decorative than informative, and like any glass surface, refract the images behind them.

Gold leaf or glass gilding, as it can be called, is a prestigious method of signing which has long been used for fascias. There are still many examples of incised gold leaf letters behind a blacked-out sheet of glass. Gilding tends to work well in shaded situations and gives lettering a 'life' that few other materials achieve.

The raw material used is almost pure gold (23 carat) in fine sheet form. The gold leaf is applied to the glass, excess moisture is blotted out and it is left to dry. A protective coat is then applied to the gold. This type of work is highly skilled and labour-intensive. It is generally used only internally or in protected locations, and can have a lifespan of about eight years if left undisturbed.

Stained glass has been used as a vehicle for translucent colours since the time of the great cathedrals. The technique of joining many small pieces together with lead probably resulted from the medieval inability to produce large sheets. It is also said to have been inspired by the oriental practice of infilling hard plaster screens with bits of coloured glass and mirror.

The range of colours and the thicknesses of glass have changed with technology. In a lighter and cheaper method, pieces of coloured glass are appliquéd on to a plain sheet of glass with adhesive, the gaps being filled with clear or black resin. Light is of course the key to the successful use of coloured glass.

Stone carving is the most ancient form of permanent lettering. The techniques of lettercutting have changed little since the time of the Romans; letters were brush-drawn on stone and then cut with a chisel. The official Roman alphabet was used for imperial and senatorial inscriptions, epitomizing the grandeur, order and uniformity of the Roman Empire. Perhaps even more magnificent were the bronze, probably gilded letters on the great triumphal arches. Nicolete Gray, in her recent book *A History of Lettering*, suggests that apart from the portrait bust, the official Roman lettering was perhaps '...the greatest original contribution of the Romans to European art'.

Stone commonly used for lettering includes slate, granite and marble. Always a popular material with designers, stone has natural qualities that cannot be successfully duplicated. It has inherent

▼ The entrance lettering for the Fisher Building, Cambridge, has been carved directly into Portland stone ashlar, adjacent to the entrance, by master craftsman Richard Kindersley.

▼ Richard Kindersley created this beautiful inscription for Sotheby's 1989 Exhibition of Decorative and Applied Arts in London. It is carved Welsh slate with the inscription painted and gilded.

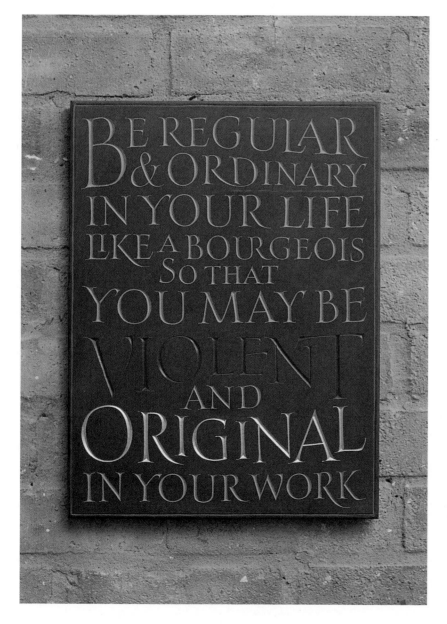

associations with permanence and strength and is extremely durable; if left to weather naturally, some types even improve in appearance. Deterioration may result from atmospheric pollution, soluble salt action, frost, wetting and drying, the rusting of ferrous metals and the effects of vegetation.

Slate

Slate is extensively used in the UK. It is stronger, harder and smoother than any other local stone. It is impervious to water and frost; its resistance is superior even to that of marble. It is often used for commemorative inscriptions and memorial tablets, and is equally suitable for nameboards, house numbers and other signs.

The cost of natural stone tends to be relatively high. Great care needs to be taken in quarrying, cutting, dressing and finishing. As with brilliant glass cutting, mistakes cannot be rectified. Stone can be polished, honed, rubbed, split, wire-sawn, heat-finished, carved, jack-hammered, sandblasted and so on. For signing purposes, stone tends to be carved or sandblasted.

Brick

Brick is seldom thought of for signing except as a support material. In the past, however, permanent

► Mr Sato designed this entrance sign to his office in Shinjuku-ku, Tokyo, using his logo of pencils sprouting like flowers from a bulb. He was especially interested in the contrast between the smooth, colourful ceramic and the rough grey concrete.

▼ This wonderful brick carving, with its sensitive design and subtle colouring, was carved *in situ*, directly into the exterior brickwork of Christie's Auction Rooms in London. It distinguishes an ordinary low-level brick building.

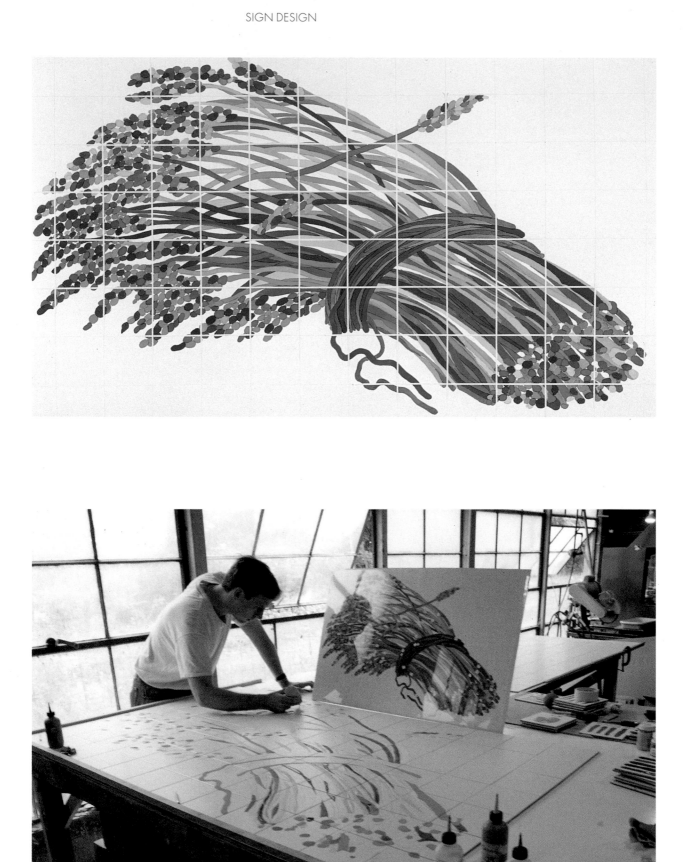

◀ Thompson's fresh bright images such as this sheaf of corn are used as decorative embellishments which also emphasize the nature of the message.

▶ Graphic artist Nick Thompson uses his talents to produce colourful handpainted ceramic tiles for Benjamin Thompson & Associates' scheme for signing Century City Marketplace in Los Angeles.

◀ A fish mural 'swims' around the corner of the building and a bird mosaic brightens the courtyard between the marketplace and a movie theatre.

▼ Large tile letters and images of vegetables, fruit, farm animals and fish, spell 'MARKETPLACE'. This wonderful freeze enlivens the environment, and, together with the other work done by BTA, has helped to regenerate this once-failing shopping centre.

lettering was literally built into brickwork, using different-coloured bricks, and bricks have on other occasions been painted to form letters. Unfortunately, many of these examples are extremely crude. Today, portable tools have made it possible to cut letters into existing brickwork, creating attractive and exciting signs.

Concrete

Casting letters into concrete has not produced the modern equivalent of the contribution made by classical Rome. However, concrete has incredible potential for the design of signs. It allows signs to be cast independently, as part of a building, or to be created on the spot. This wonderful fluid material may be formed in many shapes and a variety of finishes applied. When a sign is included

as an integral part of the design for a building, its use needs to be considered early in a project.

Ceramic

Ceramic offers one of the finest materials for signs. It is permanent, colourfast, and may be used on horizontal and vertical surfaces. Tile can serve as a decorative inset or message-carrying element on a background of contrasting material such as stucco or pavement. The vulnerability of the corners, and the tile-breaks, must both be considered by the designer. Graphics may be applied to a tile background or may be integral with it. Applications include relief numeral tiles, logo plaques and traditional mosaics.

► Chris Ludlow, of Henrion, Ludlow and Schmidt, developed the rainbow theme as a new element to revitalize the sign system for the European-wide retail chain of C&A.

6 Three signing philosophies

6 Three signing philosophies

▶ The lift lobby indicators for the
▼ headquarters of Barclays Bank
International, in London, are cast
bronze panels with the appropriate
floor number painted red. They give a
simple demonstration of how a sign
can be transformed into a sculptural
object whilst retaining its function.

This final chapter expresses, in their own words, the signing philosophies of three design professionals, each of whom work with signs in very different capacities: Richard Kindersley is a letterer and sculptor, Chris Ludlow a designer and John Wood a signmaker. Their contributions indicate the range of opinion about aspects of signing, and promote discussion and debate about signing issues.

Richard Kindersley

Richard Kindersley, born in 1939, studied lettering and sculpture first with his father, David Kindersley, and then at the Cambridge School of Art. His father had studied with Eric Gill. Since 1966 Richard Kindersley has worked in his London studio with the help of three or four assistants.

For many years, Kindersley has argued the need for a new approach to architectural lettering and signs, through his own work and public lectures to architects, designers and others. He also teaches and lectures in many art schools and associations around the country.

His outstanding work, which he describes as architectural lettering, is the best example of his philosophy towards signs. He does not support the manipulation of 'off the shelf' designs, as he puts it 'forced to fit uncomfortably into the much larger environment of architecture for which they were never designed'. When commissioned, he will look at the materials from which the building is constructed, and select materials for lettering that either echo, sympathetically respond to or even act as an exciting counterpoint to the building.

The letterform and size will flow from the requirements of the text as well as the material it is to be expressed in. Signs on buildings have many functions and levels of authority, even 'tone of voice'. Kindersley believes that, to be effective, lettering requires the same range of expression as the spoken word: it may be witty and amusing, sometimes bold and austere, and at other times simply beautiful.

The following is Richard Kindersley's personal philosophy:

Titling design for contemporary architecture is dull and stereotyped. The vast majority of buildings erected today resort to monoline sanserif typefaces, which almost invariably means Helvetica Medium. Many designers seem unable to consider appropriate alternatives. Used correctly, Helvetica is a remarkable typeface. But its undoubted adaptability is often mistaken for universal suitability.

The Pompidou Centre is a case in point. The best-known example of expressive architecture, produced in France in the mid-1970s, is titled with an apology for a sign. How could such a delightful building have inspired so feeble a response from

◄ The Cathedral Church of St Peter and St Paul, Bristol. The concrete letters, set within a monolithic concrete screen, are designed to form a bold sculptural band in front of the Cathedral.

the graphic designer? Two major British art centres come to mind as suffering from similar shortcomings: the Queen Elizabeth Hall on the South Bank, and the Barbican Centre.

On the Queen Elizabeth Hall, the Univers typeface fretted out in stainless steel humbly creeps over the strong architectural planes. The texture of the surface concrete, taken directly from the wooden shuttering, is at least one indication that the architect has looked for expressive effects, but the titling not only lacks

any reflection of this, but is virtually invisible too!

The face of a building cannot be treated in the same way as a drawing. A building is not a flat surface. On the small scale, two-dimensional typographical solutions usually work very ably for internal signing, but a title on the outside of a building must almost invariably be considered, quite differently, in terms of three dimensions, in terms of material and in terms of original letterform. It must be considered, in a word, architecturally. How much more successfully

Roman designers and craftsmen would have responded to the opportunities presented by both these two last buildings, perhaps sending great parades of elegant cast-concrete letters marching down the horizontal beams.

There seems for a long time to have been opposition among architects and designers towards expressive lettering. Inevitably such characteristics can never be wholly removed. Lettering works on several levels, containing what might be called 'archetypal' form, and to a greater

► These large concrete letters, 1.2 m high, are part of a running inscription 12m long, produced for the Richard Kindersley exhibition at London's Royal Institute of British Architects. The letterform is designed to introduce the observer to the sculptural possibilities of large letters. Once removed from the restrictions of typography, letters can be free to respond individually to one another, to the way they are made, and the materials they are made from.

▶ The Shakespeare Centre, Stratford upon Avon. The main title lettering, 560mm high, is carved directly into the brickwork. The letters are carefully considered for poise and balance, deeply incised at their edges and curved forward to the centre of the letter stroke, imparting depth and modelling to the form. The letter design is deliberately wide to enable it to be legible when viewed diagonally from the street.

or lesser extent, stylistic character. Archetypal form – the theoretical skeletal shapes of the alphabet – makes letters and words recognizable. Once actually made, letters automatically assume expressive form determined by the method used and the influence of the mind over the tool. Particular qualities can be included to direct response.

The sans serif fashion in typography, emphasizing a theoretical division of archetypal from expressive form, has had direct consequences for architectural visuals. Jan Tschichold's early typographical principles, expounded in his 'Neue Typographie' (1928) and resurrected after the war in the Swiss design school, became in the 1960s the inspiration as much for architectural graphic design as for other typographical disciplines.

The Bauhaus system soon gained widespread international recognition. Letterforms for buildings – monoline, sans serif and modular – came to be taken from the same catalogues that supplied magazine advertisements and book-jacket designs. Architectural lettering had to be straightforward, complementing the 'form follows function' doctrine of the day.

This lettering philosophy still survives intact, despite the twilight of Modernism and the exciting changes and

turns that have since occurred architecturally. We are left with the miraculous survival of what is frequently the least fit.

It cannot be too often stated that the design of lettering for architectural exteriors involves quite different considerations from the the design of type. Type has developed not only along aesthetic lines but in response to technology. A letter loses a certain amount of its distinctiveness during the process of printing and reproduction, and the type designer, counterbalancing this, builds in certain optical checks. To take these original drawings and enlarge them unaltered, to 300 mm or more, for reproduction in plastic or metal, is to ride roughshod over the art of type design and to disregard the needs of large letters, whether two- or three-dimensional.

The established conditions in which designs are processed for building titles weigh heavily against designers learning to think architecturally. Designers' skills are seldom enriched by a real understanding of, let alone intimacy with, materials. The sign manufacturers offer a limited, repetitive and commercially expedient range of materials. They long ago dropped any concern or responsibility towards ideas and innovation, selling out to pure commercialism.

Designers need to discover that there are many exciting and innovative materials that can be pressed into use as signs. Many are the materials from which buildings are made: concrete, glass, steel, wood, brick, ceramics; the list is long and stimulating. Designers find it difficult to break out of their own lack of knowledge and the sign-companies' proffered short list of the expedient. The profession of the letterer needs re-establishment, but this can only be achieved by the way in which the subject is taught.

The art of lettering has had a noble – if intricate – history. It needs to be taught properly and practised by specialists. Regulated to the position of a minor adjunct to the graphic arts, it becomes the mere manipulation of existing typefaces. The subject as a whole needs to be separated from graphic design. It should be expanded and set up as a study course of equal status in at least one of Britain's major art schools. Experiment should be the central concern, and the study of design should be inseparable from its application to materials. This is no sentimental request for a return to the romantic world of craftsmanship. It is just a plea for aesthetic and technical liberation.

161

▶ Henrion Ludlow & Schmidt have produced a system for Mitsubshi Motors to be used worldwide. These secondary directional signs are clearly identifiable with their red colour and sans serif typeface.

▼ Henrion Ludlow & Schmidt were commissioned to rethink completely the sign system for London Underground, while retaining some of the more familiar identifiers like the roundel here.

Chris Ludlow

One of the most respected and well-liked design professionals, Chris Ludlow, born in 1946, is enjoying a highly successful career. Since graduating with first-class honours in Art and Design from the London College of Printing in 1969, he has worked internationally with a number of leading design firms. He joined F.H.K. Henrion in 1977; in 1981, Henrion Ludlow and Schmidt was formed. The consultancy is known for its excellence in corporate identity design; it is one of Europe's longest-established firms in this field.

In 1984 HLS began work for the London Underground to look at their signing problems. Five years on, their scheme is underway, with one station finished and twenty-five more to be complete by summer 1990. The experience this has given HLS has established them as the leading consultancy in the design and implementation of complex signing problems. They are currently undertaking the design of the signs for London's Canary Wharf, and embarking on a review of British Rail signs.

Chris Ludlow has a clear opinion about signing. Signs span a huge range of work, from major transport undertakings to fascias for shops to individual nameplates. 'All signs give messages, of course, but the skills involved in designing a system for London Underground or a nameplate for a local accountant are worlds apart.'

Chris Ludlow is also one of the profession's most articulate spokesmen. A Fellow of the Chartered Society of Designers, Chairman of the Graphics Group and member of the Membership Committee, he also lectures in the UK and abroad. He is a member of the Society of Environmental Graphic Designers (USA). Here is his signing philosophy:

Signing is downrated in the average designer's mind. It may seem to be just a remedial task with given elements, but what appears as a mild facelift might be a hell of a lot of work in restoring health. It may be lacking in glamour and probably in superficial effect, but signing is of fundamental importance.

People don't notice signs. The research we did for the London Underground rather confirmed my worst suspicions; what they do notice is if signs are not there. The market research was almost a non-event. We couldn't even drag people into conversation. Signs really are just taken for granted. And yet they are the oil in the machinery. If they are not present then the whole thing jams up. Conversely, when the new signs were put into Victoria underground station, several people spontaneously said they thought the station had been refurbished. It hadn't.

I certainly make the distinction between signing as 'graphics' and signing as 'function'. It's as different as chalk from cheese. If you sign a development with a house style you can do a quick and pretty job. But if you are asked to look at the road signs, it will take years to do, and what then comes out will not be wildly exciting in graphic terms. But that is hardly the point. You have designed something which you hope will work.

A client's organizational procedures will also influence the actual appearance of the signs. At London Underground the Department of Signals and Electrical Engineering was responsible for the design, construction and maintenance of signs. They actually worked from a twelve-page hand-drawn and type-written 'manual' which they kept pretty close to their chests. The Operating Department (the people who run the trains) approved the schemes or requested modifications. This was until the Department of Architecture and Design received a large budget to modernize stations, whereupon they incorporated signs as part of their schemes.

The situation was chaotic. The designers didn't have the homespun manual, so they did what they thought was best. The Department of Signals and Electrical Engineering accused the designers of not sticking to the rules, so the designers said 'What rules?' and carried on regardless. The Operations Department joined in the criticism. The Department of Signals and Electrical Engineering then said, 'If the signs are not made to our specifications, then we won't maintain them.' Unfortunately the real loser was, of course, the end user.

◀ As well as signs for the London Underground, HLS also designed an identity and sign system for the shopping mall at 55 Broadway, the HQ of London Regional Transport. The brief was to be sensitive to the existing architecture in the conversion from a station concourse

163

◀ Signs designed by HLS are being installed on the main building of the Hamburg office of Beiersdorf AG, the West German pharmaceutical company. The design is intended to be used for all the company's branches in Europe.

We collaborated with London Underground in trying to solve their signing problems, but we represented the passenger. The approach we take is a problem-solving one, which doesn't allow for egocentricity. We try to maintain a very simple image: a straightforward, open, approachable style, which is not tricky or fashionable. We talk about evolution, not revolution.

We produce a scheme which works, and a signing manual for the client. Then it is a matter of getting the manual into the organization, which must be appropriately organized to do the job effectively. A manual is only as good as its interpretation. It's the people who work with it, who give it life – who make the thing succeed or fail. Problems of design 'style' are secondary. We used New Johnston for the London Underground. It would have been possible for us to spend a lot of effort getting another sanserif face with good characteristics, but it would probably be effort wasted. We believe it is better to put that energy into method of use: layout, illumination, colour and so on, to fine tune it. Designers want to re-invent the wheel all the time, just

for the sake of doing it.

We enjoy the challenge of solving complex signing problems. The importance of signs is beginning to be recognized. They have tremendous potential for influencing customer- or user-attitudes. Good signing makes friends; poor signing says an organization does not care, or has other priorities than making life easier for the user. Signing is very much an organization's 'tone of voice' and therefore a major communicator of corporate identity.

However, research into signing is urgently needed. As designers, we need to understand the scope of the problem more thoroughly than we do at present. We need information on the perception of signs, understandability, visibility, legibility, materials and so on. We need to identify key responsibilities to help clients in their staff training programmes, which include planning, and procedural skills for the implementation and management of complex sign systems. Our goal is the continued improvement of the quality of life for all users.

John Wood

Born in Melbourne, Australia, in 1930, John Wood was educated in England. He credits his early training as a chef de cuisine as giving him awareness of detail and precision of the creative process. He formed Wood and Wood, London, in 1968 and soon gained a reputation in design and manufacturing with such sign programmes as Truman's, Player's, Boot's, British Airways, Courage Breweries, STC and IBM Paris. His company is well-known for its innovative approach in using different materials and untried techniques in order to realize a particular design idea. This is his philosophy towards signmaking:

In our cities there are forests of signs. Even our countryside is becoming more and more the province of the sign. So when you come across a sign that really grabs your attention it has to be something rather special. What is that something? For me the ingredients of an outstanding sign are obvious. It has be to very well made. It also has to have been conceived as a whole, so that the graphic element and the structure and display technique all complement each other to produce an effect that is more than the sum of its parts.

In this attitude lies my whole philosophy towards signmaking: the sign is the design. There was a time when the signmaker and the designer were one and the same thing – because in one sense they are the same thing. But the signmaker became more and more the manufacturer – to the point where it is now usually a purely technical function. And the relationship between signmaker and designer has become ossified. At Wood and Wood, things are different.

Wood and Wood was founded by me in 1968. Its early experience was in the application of corporate identity design programmes in the UK and on the Continent of Europe. With the development of new manufacturing techniques, often using unconventional materials, the one-off sign started to become a profitable and high-profile part of Wood and Wood's operation. Innovations researched and developed for these specialist commissions subsequently became more widely applied in many large sign programmes. As this side of the business grew, so did our relationship with the designers who conceived and commissioned the signs. And the relationship became two-way.

In 1979, a new dimension was added to Wood and Wood with the introduction of Alphatex, an effective sign system designed to be bought 'off-the-shelf' and to be easily changed once installed. With the emphasis on high-class technical specification, graphic design and quality manufacture, the sign system business has grown rapidly, with the addition of a number of new system products helping to open up new markets around the world. Some of our sign systems have been created under the design direction of Pentagram, one of the world's foremost design consultancies, who have helped us develop the function, aesthetics and graphics. Now our sign systems are a highly successful and substantial part of the business.

THE GATE

▲ Wood and Wood won a coveted British Design and Art Directors' award for their series of pub signs for Courage Breweries in 1987.

So the set-up at Wood and Wood International Signs is different from most others in the same business, because we are, and always have been, sign makers rather than sign manufacturers. We do more than manufacture signs. We create them.

In this distinction lies our very special relationship with the design industry in the UK. The company has worked closely with design consultants and in-house designers, trying to translate creative ideas, even outrageous ones, into effective hardware, and mostly suceeding. These are the signs that designers like and want: well-engineered, using technology, materials and creativity to produce the right kind of innovation when appropriate.

Wood and Wood's relationship with the design business has given it

a special role. With great experience of how designers work, what they expect, what they do – and what they don't do – Wood and Wood has developed into more than a design-conscious signmaker. The company is now a kind of bridge between the contemporary design and sign industries.

Understanding designers is only the start. It carries through to a positive attitude to problem solving, a high regard for detail and quality, and a technical ability to innovate. And designers respond. The architectural design partner of one large London consultancy put it this way: 'They are nice, friendly people, and do it all very beautifully.'

There is substance and achievement behind this special approach to the market. In 1987, we became the first

signmaker ever to win a British Design and Art Directors' Award – hitherto the exclusive province of specialist designers and advertising agents. The award was made for a series of pub signs created for the Courage brewery. Reversing the traditional roles of designer and signmaker, Wood and Wood commissioned The Partners, a leading London design company, to execute the graphics to our specification.

Wood and Wood's effectiveness in the market-place as the designer's signmaker is supported by a high level of operational efficiency. The market for sign programmes and one-offs remains a specialist one, requiring individual service and technical expertise, coupled with a versatile and well-equipped manufacturing capability.

For special signs and sign programmes, Wood and Wood has developed an experienced and vigorous Design Technical Department, which is responsible for rationalizing and implementing all projects – especially those that present particular technical challenges.

More than twenty years of working in the sign business has confirmed my original opinion about the relationship between the sign and design. It has formed the basis for a very successful international business. It has also given me friends and contacts in design houses and architectural practices whose insights are quite different from those of industry and commerce. Being a designer's signmaker, you get the best of both worlds.

◀ Part of the 'off-the-shelf' Alphatex signing system designed by Wood and Wood.

▶ The Barbican arts and conference centre in London, with its complex multi-purpose organization, presented a challenge in directional signposting.

Further reading

Books

Adams R (1971)
Creativity in Communication
Studio Vista, London

Bartram A (1975)
Lettering in Architecture
Lund Humphries, London

Biggs J R (1968)
Basic Typography
Faber & Faber, London

Bowen Ballinger L and Ballinger R (1972)
Sign Symbol and Form
Van Nostrand Reinhold Company

Blake J (1971)
A Management Guide to Corporate Identity
Council of Industrial Design, London

Braybrooke S (1984)
The Best in Environmental Graphics
RC Publications Inc, Bethesda

Crosby T (1984)
Architecture & Poetry
Pentagram, London

Crosby T, Fletcher F and Forbes R (1970)
A Sign Systems Manual
Studio Vista, London

Effron E (1986)
Planning and Designing Lighting
Frances Lincoln Ltd, London

Follis J and Hammer D (1980)
Architectural Signing and Graphics
The Architectural Press, London

Garland K (1980)
Illustrated Graphics Glossary
Barrie and Jenkins, London

Gray N (1960)
Architectural Lettering
The Architectural Press, London

Hawes Signs
The Hawes Sign Guide
England

Henderson S and Landau R (1981)
(Michelle Feldman, ed)
Billboard Art
Angus and Robertson Publishers, London

Kindersley R and Lopes Cardozo L (1981)
Letters Slate Cut
Lund Humphries, London

Kinneir J (1980)
Words and Buildings
The Architectural Press, London

Klein L (1986)
Exhibits: Planning and Design
Madison Square Press, New York

Larwood J and Camden Hotten J (1908)
The History of Signboards from the Earliest Times to the Present Day
Chatto and Windus, London

Lawson B (1980)
How Designers Think, the Design Process Demystified
The Architectural Press, London

Manelker D R and Ewald W R (1988)
Street Graphics and the Law
Planners Press, Washington

Mason P J (1983)
A Practical Handbook of Information on Neon Signs and Cold Cathode Lighting
P J Mason & Co Ltd, London

Muller-Brockman J (1971)
A History of Visual Communication
Visual Communication Books, New York

Murray R (1983)
How to Brief Designers and Buy Print
Business Books, London

Stern R (1979)
Let There Be Neon
Harry N Abrams, New York

Sutton J (1965)
Signs in Action
Studio Vista, London

Tschichold J (1985)
Treasury of Alphabets
Omega Press, Hertfordshire

Venturi R, Scott Brown D and Izenour S (1982)
Learning from Las Vegas: the forgotten symbolism of architectural form
MIT Press, Cambridge MA

Vignelli M (1981)
Design
Rizzoli Publications Inc, New York

Journals and magazines

Designers Journal
May 1989
9 Queen Anne's Gate, London SW1

Identity
Fall 1989
New York

Octavo
no 6, 1989

Signs
no 50, July/August 1989

Technical and presentations

Arthur P (1967)
**'Who will help me find my way?
An exporation of wayfinding'**
SEGC Cranbrook Conference

Arthur P (1988)
Presentation
Canadian Architects in Industry

**Environmental Graphics
Sourcebook, Part One (1982)
Material and Techniques**
SEGD

**Manual on Uniform Traffic
Control Devices (1978)**
US Dept of Transportation

Messages
vols 1, no 2; vol 2, nos 2 and 3;
vol 3, no 1
SEGD

Frank J (1988)
Creativity
Seminar for Blueprint Workshops

Porter C (1988)
**Business and Project
Management**
Seminar for Blueprint Workshops

Glossary

acid-etching An intaglio process in which the design is etched into a surface by acid biting into the marks imposed through an acid-resistant ground such as wax. In signmaking, usually used for glass surfaces.

ambient light General level of light in an environment.

annealing Process of strengthening glass or metal by heating and then cooling.

antideflection stud A stud which protects a sheet material from deflecting under wind and weather resistance.

artwork Any matter prepared for reproduction, with full details of colour, size etc.

ascender That part of certain lowercase letters, such as b, d, f, h, which extend above the 'x' height.

blackletter Style of typeface once widely used in northern Europe, closely based on broad-nib pen style, also known as Gothic in the UK, Old English and Text Type in the US.

box sign Metal frame sign with plastic walls forming a box, often internally illuminated, and commonly used for the identification of commercial premises.

brilliant glass-cutting Faceted cutting of design into glass surface, using willow wood blade.

British Standards/Institution (BS/BSI)

calligraphy The art of fine writing. The term derives from the Greek words for 'beautiful handwriting'.

camera-ready artwork Completed artwork which is ready to go before the 'process camera'.

candela Unit of luminous intensity. A light source of 30 candelas is equivalent to a 40 Watt filament-type electric light bulb.

casting The process of reproducing a design by creating a three-dimensional form, taking a mould from it, and filling the mould with molten or liquid material such as metal or plastic which then sets solid.

cathode Negative pole or electrode.

cathode-ray tube (CRT) Standard electronic display device producing a visible image on a phosphor screen by a directed beam of electrons.

Code of Ethics Written or understood rule of proper and moral behaviour for a particular set of circumstances.

cold-cathode lamp These lamps are so-called because they obtain their electrons by 'secondary emission' from a cold cathode.

colour rendering The effect of a light source on an object's colour appearance, when compared with another reference source.

colourfast Description of an object whose colour is not affected by light/air/chemicals etc.

colourway A combination or association of specified colours/tones. A single design may be reproduced using different colourways, in, for instance, wallpaper or fabric.

computer-aided design (CAD) A design produced with the aid of a computer.

condensed letterform A standard letterform whose proportions have been altered to reduce the width of the body of the letter.

corrosion The destruction or decay of metal due to chemical or electro-chemical attack.

counter Space enclosed by closed parts of type character, such as in the letters a, b, d, e, g, o.

descender That part of certain lowercase letter, such as p, y, g, q, appearing below the 'x' height.

die-embossing A method similar to die-stamping, in which a raised image or design is embossed on the surface of metal, plastic, paper etc.

die-stamping A process in which the design is stamped out of a hard surface such as metal, so that it appears in relief.

diffuser A device to scatter light.

dressing The process of rubbing down or cleaning stone prior to polishing.

dry colour transfer Image of type, or other lettering or symbols, which is transferred from a transparent backing sheet by pressure – also called dry transfer.

edge-lighting Lighting the edge of a sheet of material (usually perspex).

Egyptian (typeface) Name at first applied to both sans serif and slab-serif typefaces by nineteenth-century founders, later reserved for slab-serifs – also known as antique.

electric discharge lamp Lamp whose light is produced by passing an electric current through a gas or vapour.

electrode A conductor emitting electrons in a gas, electrolyte or vacuum. Electrodes are either positive (the anode) or negative (the cathode).

electrolyte A solution that carries an electric current. Electrolytes may be acids, bases or salts.

electrostatic Electricity or electrically charged particle at rest.

elevation Drawing of vertical view of three-dimensional object, as opposed to a plan of the object.

ellipsoidal reflector (ER) lamp Lamp whose beam has two focal points, due to the ellipsoidal reflector placed behind the lighting filament.

embedding Process whereby lettering,

usually printed, is firmly laid in a surrounding surface, such as plastic or resin.

embossing Process of making a raised impression on board or paper, usually by die-stamping.

engraving Process, either intaglio or relief, of incising lines in a surface such as wood, metal or glass; also, the cutting of a design into a wooden or metal plate for printing.

engraving stock Plastic laminate of two coloured layers, used for an engraving process whereby the design is cut through one layer to reveal the contrasting colour below.

etching The harnessing of the chemical effect of acid on metal to produce a printable image. Glass may also be acid-etched.

expansion co-efficient The degree of change taking place due to alteration of temperature, pressure etc.

exploded view Drawing of component parts of an object, shown separately but arranged to indicate their relationship with each other.

extrusion The process of forming mouldings by forcing material, such as hot metal, through suitable dies.

fascia sign The identificational sign above a shop front or similar premises.

fibre optics The technique of transmitting light through a flexible bundle of fine, tubular fibres.

fire retardent A material or substance used to treat material in order to postpone or eliminate the possibility of fire.

flammability Potential for being set alight by fire.

flat lighting Diffused lighting that results in virtually no shadow, often with an apparent reduction in colour brightness.

flip chart Large pad of paper, generally used on an easel, bound along the top edge so that each sheet can be 'flipped' over the top.

fluorescence The emission of light, only during the absorption of radiation of a different wavelength.

fluorescent lamp A low-pressure mercury discharge lamp, producing light through the fluorescence of its coating.

foil cut and spray Method of producing a stencilled design, using lead foil as the 'mask' in which the stencil is cut. Modern techniques use plastic paint or rubber film rather than lead foil .

footcandle The unit of illumination used in the USA, expressed as lumens per square foot.

galvanize An industrial process by which iron and steel are given a coating of zinc (by galvanic action) as a preventative against rust.

Gant chart Chart originally designed by Henry L. Gant (1861-1919) used to schedule all the component tasks of a project.

gilding The application of gold leaf.

glare Any brightness in the field of view which is greater than the eye is adapted to.

glass-reinforced plastic A laminate of glass and plastic.

glassfibre A material consisting of tiny glass fibres woven into cloth and impregnated with various resins. It is known for its tensile strength and its resistance to corrosion.

gloss Shine or lustre of a surface, usually paint or polished metal.

halation The halo effect caused by a bright light source contrasting with darker surroundings.

halftone A continuous-tone subject, whether original or converted for reproduction, in contrast to a line subject.

half-tone process The photomechanical reproduction of continuous-tone originals by means of a technique which converts the image into minute graded dots, giving the appearance of continuous tone.

hardcoat Varnish, resin or similar coating which sets hard on application to a surface, giving extra protection.

hardwood Wood from deciduous trees, such as beech, oak and maple.

headline Line of type heading and identifying or titling a piece of text.

impact resistance The resilience of an object or surface when subjected to impact or surface damage.

incandescence The emission of light by the thermal excitement of a solid or liquid.

incandescent filament lamp Lamp where light is produced by heating a wire (usually tungsten) to incandescence with electricity.

irradiation See halation

kelvin Absolute temperature scale

lacquer High-gloss colourless varnish used to provide a protective surface.

laminate To beat, roll or split a substance into thin layers which are then sandwiched together.

laser Light Amplification by Stimulated Emission of Radiation, a method of producing an intense narrow beam of light.

light-emitting diode (LED) Digital display using coloured light emitted by a diode made from semiconductor materials (the colour is dependent on the material used).

legibility The degree of ease with which type can be read.

letterform The characteristic shape of an individual letter.

letterspacing The space between letters of a word.

linespacing The amount of space allocated between lines of type.

logo/type Originally several letters or a word cast as one unit of hot metal; hence also the graphic device used to identify a company.

lowercase The small letters of the alphabet (or miniscules) as opposed to capital letters.

light-reflecting displays (LRDs) Electronic display system where the display is formed by magnetic coloured discs responding to an electric current.

lumen Unit of light energy which has now superseded the footcandle.

luminance The luminous intensity of any visible surface.

lux Unit of illuminance, expressed in lumens per square metre.

manual Handbook of instructions.

margin Blank area surrounding printed matter.

matrix Pattern mould or arrangement of cells used in electronic display systems.

matt Dull, lustreless surface.

mill finish Untreated metal finish.

mock-up Rough visual presentation of proposed design.

modern (typeface) Class of typefaces dating back to the late eighteenth century, characterized by fine hairlines and unbracketed serifs.

neon An inert gas.

offset photolithography (offset litho, offset printing) Usual commercial form of photolithography, in which an inked image is transferred to a rubber blanket, then to paper.

off-the-peg Readymade.

old face (type) (US old style) Class of typefaces dating from the early sixteenth century.

open front lettering Metal-channelled letters where the channel holds a glass lighting tube for night illumination.

optical balance Visually pleasing appearance of large lettering that has been adjusted to take its magnified size into account.

phosphor Fluorescent substance used to coat the inside of cathode-ray tubes and fluorescent lamps.

photocomposition Preferred term for any system of typesetting by photographic means, but also known as phototypesetting and, inaccurately, as photosetting.

photometer Instrument for measuring intensity of light.

pigment Colouring-matter in a paint or dye.

pictogram Pictorial representation of an object.

pouncing The process of transferring a design, using dusting powder, from one surface to another, such as from paper to glass.

presentation pack A compilation of visual material intended to show design suggestions to a client.

press-forming Method of shaping plastic. It is heated, then vacuum-formed over a mould.

pressure-sensitive marking See 'transfer lettering'

process camera Camera constructed especially for photomechanical reproduction processes, also called a graphic arts camera.

prototype An early three-dimensional version of a design, usually made to see whether it will work or not.

retail identity Usually a visual identity for a retail outlet or store.

Roman (typeface) Very general term covering all typefaces deriving from humanistic manuscripts, as distinct from blackletter (gothic). Also used to distinguish non-italic letterforms.

sign pans Moulded sign panels.

sandblasting The process of blasting a material such as glass with a directional, pressurized stream of fine sand particles.

sanserif Any typeface that lacks serifs, and that does not usually differentiate between 'thick' and 'thin' strokes.

screenprinting Method of printing by forcing ink through a thin fabric or metal mesh screen. The image is formed by a stencil formed photographically or manually on the screen.

scrim An open-weave fabric, usually woven from polyester when used for signing.

SEGD Society of Environmental Graphic Designers, a US-based professional group.

sheet steel Generally used in signing with a coating of either lead or zinc.

signing schedule An inventory listing the total number and location of signs within a system, together with the information to be given on each sign.

softwood Wood coming from coniferous trees, such as pine and cedar.

split-flap message Electronic signing system using motor-driven rotating discs with a number of flaps revealing individual letters or words.

spotlight Lamp throwing a concentrated beam of light on to a small area.

squeegee Screenprinting implement with rubber blade used for pulling ink across the surface of the screen.

stencil Thin sheet of card, metal or another suitable material, into which a design is cut, so that when colour is applied to the stencil surface, it prints through the cut area onto the surface below.

step-down transformer A transformer which delivers a low voltage to the output, as in low-voltage lighting.

substrate Layer underneath the main surface of a material.

template Thin board or metal plate cut to the shape of a design and used as a pattern to cut or draw around.

thermoforming The process of forming by the use of heat.

transflective Term used to describe liquid crystal displays which combine their reflective properties with the ability to transmit light.

transfer lettering Image of type or other lettering which is transferred from a transparent backing sheet by pressure; also called 'dry transfer'.

transformer A device which changes the incoming (primary) voltage and delivers a different (secondary) voltage to the output.

transitional (typeface) Class of typefaces dating from the mid eighteenth century, having somewhat finer serifs and hairlines than 'old face' but not to the extent of 'modern'.

transmission The process by which incident (arriving) light passes through and leaves a medium, modified according to the surface.

typeface Letterforms designed with particular characteristics to unite them within one alphabet or typeface. Typefaces are generally described as 'serif' or 'sanserif', and each typeface contains individual elements distinguishing it from all others.

typesetting See phototypesetting.

typography Originally (and still to some extent in the US) the art and technique of working with type. In the UK it has come to mean, specifically, layout of typeset and accompanying graphic matter for reproduction.

vacuum-forming Shaping thin plastic sheeting by means of a vacuum.

value engineering The cost-based assessment of material components, with the aim of getting the best value for money.

visual display terminal (VDT) A device incorporating a keyboard, logic system and cathode-ray tube (CRT), connected to a computer and used to display alphanumeric or graphic information stored in a computer; also used to key in queries so that the result of an interrogation may be viewed on screen.

visual display unit (VDU) A cathode-ray tube (CRT) which may be used as part of a VDT or to stand alone as an information device.

visual identity The identity of a company as presented visually.

vitreous enamel Coloured glass, powdered and fused, used as decoration or as a surface on which to print.

wavelength The distance between one peak or crest of a wave and the next corresponding peak or crest; can be applied to heat, sound or other electro-magnetic waves.

wordspacing The space between words to distinguish one from the next.

'x' height The mean height of lower-case characters which have neither ascenders nor descenders.

Index

Picture acknowledgements
The publishers and author gratefully acknowledge the following for permission to use their material in this book: BDP (70/71); Jim Bodoh (18, 23, 44, 45, 119, 134, 144 *top*, 149 *bottom*); Antony Broadbent (104/5, 108); Maurice Broughton Associates (124); Carbone Smolan Associates (37 above [Photo: Ave Pildas]; 42, 43 [Photos: Mark Greenberg]; 37 below, 76, 98, 99, 100, 101 [Photos: Philippe de Potestad]); Chermayeff and Geismar (19, 24, 25, 49, 54, 55 *bottom*, 56, 135); Conran Design Group (13, 51 *bottom*, 58, 72/73); © Stephanie Couturier/Archipress (76, 130); Design House (35, 39, 46, 117, 137); Douglas Doolittle (7, 21 top, 21 *bottom*); Fitch RS/Ian McKinnell (61, 74); Alan Fletcher of Pentagram Design (22 *bottom*); Ken Garland (47); Barbara Gladstone Gallery, New York (127, 129); Goddard and Gibbs (150); Fritz Gottschalk, Gottschalk and Ash International, Zurich (52, 102/3); Hawes Signs (78 *top*, 128, 148); Henrion, Ludlow and Schmidt (8, 68, 69, 141, 157, 162, 163, 164); Igarashi Studio, photograph courtesy Mitsumsasa Fujitsuka (77, 144 *bottom*); Richard Kindersley (151, 152, 153 *bottom*, 158, 159, 160, 161); Robert Landau, Los Angeles (27, 120); Lloyd Northover (14, 148); John McConnell and Ralph Selby of Pentagram Design, photograph courtesy of Dennis Gilbert (140); Ian McKinnell (74 *top and bottom*); Pentagram Design Group (66/67, 82/83); Coco Raynes (75, 132, 147); Richard Roger's Partnership, photograph courtesy ARCAID (1180; U.G. Sato (153 *top*); Mitzi Sims (12, 15, 17, 20, 36, 40, 41, 48 *top*, 50, 53, 78 *bottom*, 79, 107, 109, 110, 110, 111, 112, 113, 114, 115, 116, 121, 122, 123, 126, 136, 138, 143, 145, 146, 149 *top*); SOM (84, 86, 89, 94, 95, 96, 97); Benjamin Thompson Associates (28, 29, 30, 154, 155); Tilney Lumsden Shane (48 *bottom*); Jeremy Tilston from Smith and Milton (22 *top*); Trickett Associates (62/63, 64, 65); Vignelli Associates (10, 16, 26, 51 *top*); Weber Design (80 *top*, 80 *bottiom*, 81); Wood and Wood (165, 166, 167); Hiroshi Yoshioka (32/3, 38).